Decolonising African University Knowledges, Volume 1

This timely work investigates the possibility of unyoking and decolonising African university knowledges from colonial relics. It claims that academics from socially, politically, and geographically underprivileged communities in the South need to have their voices heard outside of the global power structure.

The book argues that African universities need a relevant curriculum that is related to the cultural and environmental experiences of diverse African learners in order to empower themselves and transform the world. It is written by African scholars and is based on theoretical and practical debates on the epistemological complexities affecting and afflicting diversity in higher education in Africa. It examines who are the primary custodians of African university knowledges, as well as how this relates to forms of exclusion affecting women, the differently abled, the rural poor, and ethnic minorities, as well as the significance of the Fourth Industrial Revolution in the future of African universities. The book takes an epistemological approach to university teaching and learning, addressing issues such as decolonisation and identity, social closure and diversity disputes, and the obstacles that come with the neoliberal paradigm.

The book will be necessary reading for academics, scholars, and postgraduate students in the fields of Sociology of Education, decolonising education, Inclusive Education, and Philosophy of Education, as it resonates with existing discourses.

Amasa P. Ndofirepi holds a PhD in Philosophy of Education and is currently an Associate Professor of Philosophy and History of Education at Sol Plaatje University and a Research Associate at the Ali Mazrui Centre for Higher Education Studies, University of Johannesburg. He has extensive experience in teacher education, previously worked at various higher education institutions in Zimbabwe and South Africa and has research interests in higher education studies from a philosophical perspective.

Felix Maringe is a Professor of Higher Education and Head of the School of Education at the University of the Witwatersrand in South Africa. He researches issues of social justice in the Internationalisation and Globalisation of Higher Education. Felix is widely published in refereed journals and has six books to his credit.

Simon Vurayai is a post-doctoral research fellow at the University of Johannesburg in South Africa. He holds a PhD in the Sociology of Education. He is also a lecturer in the Sociology of Education at Great Zimbabwe University. His research interests are gender studies, social justice, problems in education, sociology of knowledge, sociology of mass media, sociology of development and poverty.

Gloria Erima is a post-doctoral fellow at the department of Education and Curriculum Studies at the University of Johannesburg in South Africa. Her research interest is centred around issues of social justice in education. She obtained her PhD in Education Leadership and Management at the University of the Witwatersrand in South Africa.

Routledge Research in Decolonizing Education

The *Routledge Research in Decolonizing Education* series aims to enhance our understanding and facilitate ongoing debates, research and theory relating to decolonization, decolonizing education and the curriculum, and postcolonialism in education. The series is international in scope and is aimed at upper-level and postgraduate students, researchers, and research students, as well as academics and scholars.

Books in the series include:

Decolonizing Transcultural Teacher Education through Participatory Action Research
Dialogue, Culture, and Identity
Jean Kirshner and George Kamberelis

Global South Scholars in the Western Academy
Harnessing Unique Experiences, Knowledges, and Positionality in the Third Space
Edited by Staci B. Martin and Deepra Dandekar

Interrogating the Relations between Migration and Education in the South
Migrating Americas
Edited by Ligia (Licho) López López, Ivón Cepeda-Mayorga, and María Emilia Tijoux

The Languaging of Higher Education in the Global South
De-Colonizing the Language of Scholarship and Pedagogy
Edited by Sinfree Makoni, Cristine G. Severo, Ashraf Abdelhay, and Anna Kaiper-Marquez

Decolonising African University Knowledges, Volume 1
Voices on Diversity and Plurality
Edited by Amasa P. Ndofirepi, Felix Maringe, Simon Vurayai, and Gloria Erima

Decolonising African University Knowledges, Volume 2
Challenging the Neoliberal Mantra
Edited by Amasa P. Ndofirepi, Felix Maringe, Simon Vurayai, and Gloria Erima

For more information about the series, please visit www.routledge.com/Routledge-Research-in-Decolonizing-Education/book-series/RRDE

Decolonising African University Knowledges, Volume 1
Voices on Diversity and Plurality

Edited by Amasa P. Ndofirepi,
Felix Maringe, Simon Vurayai,
and Gloria Erima

LONDON AND NEW YORK

First published 2023
by Routledge
4 Park Square, Milton Park, Abingdon, Oxon OX14 4RN

and by Routledge
605 Third Avenue, New York, NY 10158

Routledge is an imprint of the Taylor & Francis Group, an informa business

© 2023 selection and editorial matter Amasa P. Ndofirepi, Felix Maringe, Simon Vurayai, and Gloria Erima; individual chapters, the contributors

The right of Amasa P. Ndofirepi, Felix Maringe, Simon Vurayai, and Gloria Erima to be identified as the authors of the editorial material, and of the authors for their individual chapters, has been asserted in accordance with sections 77 and 78 of the Copyright, Designs and Patents Act 1988.

All rights reserved. No part of this book may be reprinted or reproduced or utilised in any form or by any electronic, mechanical, or other means, now known or hereafter invented, including photocopying and recording, or in any information storage or retrieval system, without permission in writing from the publishers.

Trademark notice: Product or corporate names may be trademarks or registered trademarks, and are used only for identification and explanation without intent to infringe.

British Library Cataloguing-in-Publication Data
A catalogue record for this book is available from the British Library

Library of Congress Cataloging-in-Publication Data
Names: Ndofirepi, Amasa, editor. | Maringe, Felix, editor. | Vurayai, Simon, editor. | Erima, Gloria, editor.
Title: Decolonising African university knowledges. volume 1 : voices on diversity and plurality / edited by Amasa P. Ndofirepi, Felix Maringe, Simon Vurayai and Gloria Erima.
Description: First Edition. | New York : Routledge, 2023. | Series: Routledge Research in Decolonising Education | Includes bibliographical references and index.
Identifiers: LCCN 2022020372 (print) | LCCN 2022020373 (ebook) | ISBN 9781032132273 (Hardback) | ISBN 9781032132280 (Paperback) | ISBN 9781003228233 (eBook)
Subjects: LCSH: Education--Decolonization. | Education, Higher--Social aspects--Africa. | Universities and colleges--Social aspects--Africa. | Education and globalization--Africa. | Cultural pluralism--Study and teaching (Higher)--Africa. | Inclusive education--Africa.
Classification: LCC LB2362.A3 D43 2023 (print) | LCC LB2362.A3 (ebook) | DDC 378.6--dc23/eng/20220701
LC record available at https://lccn.loc.gov/2022020372
LC ebook record available at https://lccn.loc.gov/2022020373

ISBN: 978-1-032-13227-3 (hbk)
ISBN: 978-1-032-13228-0 (pbk)
ISBN: 978-1-003-22823-3 (ebk)

DOI: 10.4324/9781003228233

Typeset in Times New Roman
by SPi Technologies India Pvt Ltd (Straive)

Contents

	List of Illustrations	vii
	List of Abbreviations	viii
	List of Contributors	x

1   Gender, Disability and Rurality: Decoding the
Themes in the African University Milieu   1
AMASA P. NDOFIREPI

2   Reflection on Disability (and) Educational Justice in
Africa's Structurally Unjust Society During the
COVID-19 Pandemic Lockdown: Africa's Structurally
Unjust Society During Lockdown   8
ERASMUS MASITERA

3   Improving Processes, Practices and Structures in South
African Higher Education: Voices of Students
with Disabilities   22
SIBONOKUHLE NDLOVU

4   Social Justice in Higher Education: A Quest for Equity,
Inclusion and Epistemic Access   39
TSEDISO MICHAEL MAKOELLE

5   Decolonising African University Teaching by Unyoking
Deaf Culture from Disability   52
MARTIN MUSENGI

6   Theorising Feminist Voices in the Curriculum in an African
University   68
BEATRICE AKALA

vi *Contents*

7 Knowledge Democracy and Feminist Epistemic
Struggle in African Universities 84
SIMON VURAYAI

8 Globalisation and Commodification of Knowledge
Liberating Women's Academic Achievements from
Conventional Global Power Hierarchies 103
ZVISINEI MOYO

9 The Place of Universities in Africa in the Global
Information Society: A Critique 117
J. KUNDAI CHINGARANDE AND CLYTON DEKEZA

10 Gender, Disability, Rurality, and Social Injustice in
the African University: Opportunities Going Forward 126
AMASA P. NDOFIREPI

Afterword 132
YUSEF WAGHID

Index 134

Illustrations

Table

3.1 Summary of the basic professional knowledge in education   25

Figures

4.1 Stratified representation of reality in institutions
of higher learning   42
4.2 Dyson's schematic representation of inclusion discourses and
underlying social justice views   42
4.3 Higher education institution inclusive structure   47

Abbreviations

AAC&U	Association of American Colleges and Universities
APA	American Psychological Association
ASL	American Sign Language
COVID-19	Coronavirus Disease of 2019
DHET	Department of Higher Education and Training
DoE	Department of Education
DPI	Disabled People's International
DU	Disability Unit
EMIS	Educational Management Information System
HE	Higher Education
ICD	International Classification of Disease
ICDH	International Classification of Impairments, Disabilities and Handicaps
ICT	Information and Communications Technology
ILD	Individuals Living with a Disability
MoPSE	Ministry of Primary and Secondary Education
OECD	Organisation for Economic Co-operation and Development
OVCs	Orphans and Vulnerable Children
NRF	National Research Foundation
PhD	Doctor of Philosophy
RSA	Republic of South Africa
STEM	Science, Technology, Engineering and Mathematics
UNCRPD	United Nations Convention on the Rights of People with Disabilities
UDHRC	Universal Declaration of Human Rights Charter
UFS	University of the Free State
UGHE	University of Global Health
UJ	University of Johannesburg
UKZN	University of KwaZulu-Natal
UL	University of Limpopo
ULK	Kigali Independent University
UMP	University of Mpumalanga
UNESCO	United Nations Educational, Scientific and Cultural Organisation

Abbreviations ix

UN SDGs	United Nations Sustainable Development Goals
USA	United States of America
VC	Vice-Chancellor
WHO	World Health Organisation
ZIMCHE	Zimbabwe Council for Higher Education
ZOU	Zimbabwe Open University

Contributors

Beatrice Akala is a Research Associate, Education and Curriculum Studies Department, University of Johannesburg. Dr Akala is a multidisciplinary scholar with scholarship interests in social justice, policy analysis, gender, higher education research and curriculum implementation policies.

J. Kundai Chingarande is a lecturer at Ezekiel Guti University, Department of Education and leadership Development. She teaches Sociology of Education modules at undergraduate level. Ms Chingarande is a PhD student with North West University, South Africa. Her research interests include Gender and Education, Quality Education, Children's Rights and Education.

Clyton Dekeza teaches Sociology of education modules at undergraduate and postgraduate levels at Great Zimbabwe University. Dr Dekeza holds the following qualifications: DED Sociology of Education UNISA (2018), MED Sociology of Education UZ (2005), BA Gen UNISA (2018). His research interests include social inequalities and education, Culture and Education, OVCs and education.

Tsediso Michael Makoelle is one of the recipients of the prestigious Nelson Mandela scholarship to the United Kingdom (UK). He holds the degrees of Doctor of Philosophy (PhD) in Inclusive Education from the University of Manchester, UK and a Doctor of Education (DEd) in Education Management and Leadership from University of South Africa (UNISA). He has written and published extensively on the topics of inclusive education.

Erasmus Masitera (posthumous) held a Bachelor of Arts in degree in philosophy, a Masters in Philosophy and a doctorate in the same field. Masitera was a well-published scholar in the fields of applied ethics, existentialism and metaethics. He lectured African and contemporary philosophy at Great Zimbabwe University.

Zvisinei Moyo is a lecturer in the Division of Educational Leadership, Policy and Skills in the School of Education at the University of the Witwatersrand. Her current research interests include education leadership, women in education leadership, indigenous research methodologies, social justice and gender issues.

Contributors xi

Martin Musengi is Associate Professor of Deaf and Special Needs Education at Great Zimbabwe University (GZU). Currently he is Director of Quality Assurance and Academic Planning at GZU. He is a teacher of the deaf since 1986, his abiding research interests are in Deaf Education from school to higher education levels.

Sibonokuhle Ndlovu is a post-doctoral research fellow at Ali Mazrui Centre for higher education studies, at the University of Johannesburg. She is a recipient of the National Research Foundation Innovation Post-Doctoral Fellowship, who has several publications around disability issues and the inclusion of students with disabilities in South African higher education.

Amasa P. Ndofirepi holds a PhD in Philosophy of Education and is currently an Associate Professor of Philosophy and History of Education at Sol Plaatje University and a Research Associate at the Ali Mazrui Centre for Higher Education Studies, University of Johannesburg. He has extensive experience in teacher education, previously worked at various higher education institutions in Zimbabwe and South Africa and has research interests in higher education studies from a philosophical perspective.

Simon Vurayai is a post-doctoral research fellow at the University of Johannesburg in South Africa. He holds a PhD in Sociology of Education. He is also a lecturer in the Sociology of Education in the Department of Educational Foundations at Great Zimbabwe University, Zimbabwe. His research interests are, gender studies, and sociology of knowledge.

Yusef Waghid is a Distinguished African philosopher of education at the Stellenbosch University, South Africa.

1 Gender, Disability and Rurality

Decoding the Themes in the African
University Milieu

Amasa P. Ndofirepi

Universities in every society are torchbearers. The centrality of the role of university education as institutions of higher learning is, in practice, as prime springs of higher knowledge and skills—crucial and indispensable drivers of the economy (Ndofirepi & Cross, 2017, p. 1). However African university knowledges are under siege. The colonisation of the land goes hand-in-hand with the geopolitics of knowledge, specifically the domination of Eurocentric thought that classifies regions and people around the world as underdeveloped economically and mentally (Mignolo, 2011). The dawn and the unfolding of Eurocentric modernity through colonialism and imperialism unleashed a particularly racial ethnocentric attitude that led European colonialists to question the very humanity of African people, including their ways of knowing (Ndlovu-Gatsheni, 2016). Is this not *"epistemological imperialism"* (Osha, 2011, p. 152), or *"epistemicide"* (Ramose, 2003), or *"epistemological authoritarianism"* (Kaphagawani, 1998), or *"epistemic injustice"* (Fricker, 2009)? Did this not lead to the entrapment of African university knowledges into the tentacles of cultural imperialism and gross inequalities (gender, racial, class, ethnic, etc.) from which it should be unyoked? What guidance should Africa get from her regiment of academics as torchbearers?

For decades after many African states gained political independence, there have been debates on how their universities should break from the yoke of the erstwhile colonisers as manifested in content, research, technology, and language. It is now time for African universities to turn a blind eye to the "singularisation of human diversity by being forced onto a singular track of historical 'progress' grounded on an emulation and/or mimicry of European historicity" (Serequeberhan, 2002, p. 67). African universities need a relevant curriculum that is related to the cultural and environmental experiences of diverse African learners to empower themselves and transform the world as well. Should such a curriculum come from the erstwhile colonisers? Many of the theories that originated in the West do not fit the situation in Africa and are not suitable for African children, students, scholars and researchers. There is a need for a paradigm shift regarding the language of instruction in Africa since theories built on immigrants and minority populations in the West do not apply in the local context (Brock-Utne, 2017). Is this not what Rahnema (2001) calls *"paradigmatic tyranny"*? African languages in higher

DOI: 10.4324/9781003228233-1

2   Amasa P. Ndofirepi

education have been relegated to the periphery and this has an impact on disseminating knowledge produced, hence the need for a *decolonisation of the mind* (wa Thiong'o, 1998)—African academics also have local audiences to write for. To fulfil this social responsibility, the use of African languages in curriculum and research becomes handy (Kamwendo, 2014). How then should African universities unyoke themselves from linguicide?

There is so much the Western world could learn from Africa, but that will only happen when Africa looks to herself, her history, traditions and culture and does not allow herself to be subjugated to the global governance of education (Brock-Utne, 2017); a matter of "African know thyself" (Mungwini, 2017, n.p.). What then are the implications of globalisation and commodification of knowledge to an African university? Research by Africans for Africans as a tool for fighting human problems has been denigrated in higher education. There have been various initiatives to promote research and knowledge production in the African higher education sector since the 1970s. Despite the attempts, why is it that in terms of research output Africa is still the lowest compared to other regions (Jowi & Mbwette, 2017)? Is this not the time to rescue African knowledges from extinction?

Apart from curriculum and research being under siege in higher education in Africa, a variety of other forms of social exclusion has been ignored. The exclusion of individuals based on gender, ethnicity, technology, rurality and disability that can, in some part, be traced to the workings of colonialism, may have impeded knowledge production in higher education in Africa. Empirical research has revealed disturbing sub-texts of racism, classism and sexism within the academy and the endemic structures that marginalised women and Black men (Naicker, 2013). Globally, few students living with disabilities progress to higher education. Even those few students who make it to higher education continue to face challenges (Mutanga, 2018). There is no doubt that such a group can make considerable contributions to knowledge and curriculum if inclusive avenues for them are opened. Alwy and Schech (2004) admit that relatively small, clearly defined ethnic groups have accumulated an advantage over the majority of the national population in terms of higher education infrastructure and resources. Given the various forms of exclusion, then who are the principal custodians of African university knowledges? Do women, the disabled, the rural poor, the marginalised ethnic groups also belong to this category? What role does the fourth industrial revolution play to unyoke the knowledges trapped by the technological divide and other forms of exclusion?

This book aims to problematise the extent to which it is possible to unyoke and decolonise African university knowledges. In Chapter 2, Erasmus Masitera explores the African disability justice discourse by appropriating some African moral views into the higher education discourse. In this presentation, he seeks to establish the authentic African moral perception of disability. Firstly, he situates the argument within the Ubuntu metaphysical conceptions of what it means to be human. Secondly, he contends that through the notion of communal living of African society, people living with

Gender, Disability and Rurality 3

disabilities are accepted, respected and tolerated through the relational and inclusive attitudes that emanate from African moral thinking. Thirdly, by drawing views from the first and second positions, the chapter proposes moral citizen education which institutions of higher learning have to supply. The chapter proposes a moral education that propagates a sense of Ubuntu responsibility and obligation for both disabled and non-disabled as a way of moving towards mutual respect and recognition. Lastly, a plea is made for appropriating the Ubuntu moral values in contemporary ways of living.

Sibonokuhle Ndlovu's Chapter 3, "Improving processes, practices and structures in South African higher education: Voices of students with disabilities", presents the voices of students with disabilities on improving the structures and practices in an institution of higher education in South Africa. Motivated by the continued exclusion of students with disabilities in learning institutions despite their increased access to higher education, resulting in high dropout, delayed and low throughput by the particular students, the author collected data through interviews conducted with students with disabilities who studied the professional degrees of Medicine, Law and Education at an institution of higher education. The specific structures to be improved were physical structures such as the built environment and transport as well as the practice of classroom teaching. A conceptual framework built on theoretical concepts drawn from decolonial theory and critical disability theory was used to inform the study. The findings revealed that the students with disabilities' voice on improving the structures and practices were a partnership among responsible stakeholders, adequate funding, self-advocacy by students with disabilities and total transformation of the system of higher education. The chapter concludes that the voice of students with disabilities could improve the specific structures and practices in higher education because they have a lived experience of disabilities.

In Chapter 4, "Social justice in higher education: A quest for equity, inclusion and epistemic access", T. M. Makoelle begins by arguing how traditionally disability centres at universities were historically established to offer support to students with disabilities and special educational needs. However, the implementation of inclusive education has presented the universities with a mammoth task of totally overhauling their teaching and learning processes and procedures to have students with disabilities and special educational needs educated alongside their peers in an inclusive and less restrictive educative environment. Therefore, he proposes the implementation of inclusive education in higher education by calling for the renewed strategies of academic planning, pedagogical and curriculum design, infrastructure redesign, deployment of assistive technologies, and the development of an inclusive culture which may widen and broaden the participation of diverse students in teaching and learning. The chapter, through a critical realism lens, critically analyses the transition of a university towards inclusive education within the South African context. Using critical analysis of the literature, the chapter unmasks the underlying relational mechanism for inclusion and exclusion within the framework of notions of epistemic access and dealing with

4 *Amasa P. Ndofirepi*

organisational barriers for inclusion, epistemology and pedagogical choices, cognitive justice, decolonisation and indigenisation of curriculum as well as the knowledge economy.

Martin Musengi, in Chapter 5, titled "Decolonising African university teaching by unyoking deaf culture from disability", argues that universities have tended to filter their understanding of deafness through a pathologic model that views it as a disability in need of remediation. Most university systems believe that deaf people are, at least in a physiological sense, inferior to hearing people as they patronise deaf aspirants when it comes to university education. Universities usually assess the extent to which their curricula can remediate deaf students so that they learn the same things as hearing students. This approach of viewing deafness as a communication disability in a largely hearing world is colonial as it attempts to assimilate them to a dominant hearing culture. It is the antithesis of the United Nations (UN) Sustainable Development Goal (SDG) 4 with its thrust of celebrating diversity and providing quality, inclusive education for all—including those who are deaf. African universities, with their background of protest and struggle against colonialism, should be better placed to put in place curricula that recognise and celebrate diversity. This chapter analyses how African university curricula remain in colonial mode concerning learners who ought to be considered culturally Deaf rather than disabled. The chapter discusses the philosophy and practices that colonise education for this group of learners. It also examines principles, strategies and practices that can be used to reverse and decolonise university education in Africa. The chapter also proposes curricula considerations that could propel African university education to the forefront of showcasing inclusive education as a construct for liberation rather than domestication, for celebrating diversity rather than assimilating, and for decolonising rather than colonising others.

The question of feminist philosophy is explored by Beatrice Akala in Chapter 6, titled "Theorising feminist voices in the curriculum in an African university" in which she discusses the place of gender skewing in leadership, access, and course selection as women and girls continue to experience discrimination in education in general. Apart from personal preference, their poor representation in Science, Technology, Engineering and Mathematics (STEM) subjects and courses can be attributed to how the curriculum has been designed to systematically allocate women's insignificant positions in textbooks and other learning materials (Yenika-Agbaw, 2014). The chapter explores how women's voices have been subliminal in education discourses, more so in curriculum and knowledge production. The arguments in the chapter are premised on the fact that knowledge and power intersect at a fundamental level. The chapter argues that women are an important group that should not be ignored in the academy; therefore, their voices should be appropriated to form an integral part of the curriculum. The chapter is based on a critical exploration of relevant theories (feminist theorists and post-structuralism) and secondary literature to augment its position.

Gender, Disability and Rurality 5

In Chapter 7, "Knowledge democracy and the feminist epistemic struggle in African universities", Simon Vurayai debates the extent to which feminist epistemic struggles have been regarded as insignificant by men in various professional powerbases. Feminist epistemologists have long accused men of monopolising knowledge and discounting women's contributions to the various fields of knowledge. The author avers that African academics have been subjected to epistemological discrimination for several decades compared to other regions of the globe. There is no doubt that both men and women have been, and are still, victims of this prejudice. Feminists such as Spender and Friedan have deplored the tenacity of the sexist definition of knowledge and how men engross the production, dissemination, and custodianship of knowledge in the Global North. Women have been denied access to, and participation in, certain fields of knowledge. History has it that women have realised this disparity and have since contested and protested in some way. When transposed to Africa, the chapter attests that women academics suffer more from this bigotry than their male counterparts. The genesis of the feminist epistemic struggle is explored and the state of gender and knowledge democracy in African universities is given a critical eye. The chapter proffers the strategies that African women academics should persistently employ to challenge their relegation and stand their ground that they have a right to be knowers and custodians of knowledge.

In Chapter 8, Zvisinei Moyo's "Globalisation and commodification of knowledge liberating women's academic achievements from conventional global power hierarchies" analyses the gender equity concerns in the marketisation and commodification of higher education in Zimbabwe. Utilising a variety of written sources including demographic statistical distribution of population and schools, funding of higher education as well as political, economic and social characteristics, this chapter argues that existing challenges in higher education have worsened the power hierarchies, disabling ways through which women acquire the means to fund their tertiary education. The treatment of higher education as a traded commodity to be retailed by academic institutions and to be purchased by consumers has added yet another layer of economic destitution and desperation to the endless list of deep-seated gender inequalities. Hence, marketisation and commodification of higher education in Zimbabwe has been one of the products of mechanisms designed to enforce an elite-driven, self-enrichment project disguised as indigenisation. The post-colonial state inherited colonial structures of industrial capitalism to escalate social inequalities. Although the chapter focuses on a single country within the African context, it raises important implications for research, policy-making and practice in higher education. It also has the potential to serve as a springboard to develop more broad-based, multiple-method, large sample and comparison studies that focus on further documenting gender inequalities entrenched in the marketisation and commodification of higher education and, more importantly, on documenting progress made to address these concerns.

6 *Amasa P. Ndofirepi*

The 21st-century society is a knowledge society characterised by the introduction and advancement in technology, and the new technologies have brought significant changes in the way education is conducted. In Chapter 9, entitled "The place of universities in Africa in the global information society: A critique", K. Chingarande and C. Dekeza explore the link between rurality and the digital divide and its attendant problems for the African university student. In education, e-learning was adopted and its usage by institutions of learning, including universities, has surged in the recent past due to COVID-19 lockdowns. The concept of the technological divide refers to the unequal development of new technologies between different places and regions. It is acknowledged that some places or regions are highly developed technologically, for instance, the Global North, whereas the Global South lags behind. There is also a digital divide between urban and rural, a divide that is tilted against the rural areas. The technological inequality advantages some learners who can access the new technologies, while learners in the Global South—and particularly in rural areas—are on the receiving end. To interrogate this technological dichotomy and its ramifications on the education of learners, Wallerstein's (1974) World System theory on global inequality was applied in the discourse. The chapter focuses specifically on challenges faced by students in African universities in accessing the new technologies. It emerged that students in African universities, particularly those with a rural background, are not catered for in adopting e-learning as a mode of instruction and that strategies that take disadvantaged learners on board should be sought.

Amasa Ndofirepi, in Chapter 10 entitled "Gender, disability, rurality, and social injustice in the African university: Opportunities going forward", wraps up the book volume by linking the discourses on gender, disability, and rurality which are considered social justice concerns as universities in Africa attempt to settle for decolonised knowledge production and dissemination. The chapter draws on the deliberations in the book chapters and synergises the conclusive positions of the authors to discuss the opportunities going forward in African universities in the 1st century.

References

Alwy, A., & Schech, S. (2004). Ethnic inequalities in education in Kenya. *International Education Journal, 5*(2), 266–274.

Brock-Utne, B. (2017). Decolonisation of knowledge in the African University. In M. Cross & A. Ndofirepi (Eds.), *Knowledge and change in African universities* (pp. 161–181). Sense Publishers.

Fricker, M. (2009). *Epistemic injustice: Power and the ethics of knowing.* Oxford University Press.

Jowi, J. O., & Mbwette, T. (2017). The role of research centres and networks. In J. Knight & E. T. Woldegiorgis (Eds.), *Regionalization of African higher education: Progress and prospects* (pp. 113–134). Sense Publishers.

Gender, Disability and Rurality 7

Kamwendo, G. (2014). Language policies of South African accredited journals in humanities and social sciences: Are they speaking the language of transformation? *Alternation, 21*(2), 207–222.

Kaphagawani, D. N. (1998). What is African philosophy? In P. H. Coetzee & A. P. J. Roux (Eds.), *The African philosophy reader* (pp. 86–98). Routledge.

Mignolo, W. D. (2011). *The darker side of Western modernity: Global futures, decolonial options*. Duke University Press.

Mungwini, P. (2017). "African know thyself": Epistemic injustice and the quest for liberative knowledge. *International Journal of African Renaissance Studies - Multi-, Inter- and Transdisciplinarity, 12*(2), 5–18. doi:10.1080/18186874.2017.1392125

Mutanga, O. (2018). Inclusion of students with disabilities in South African higher education. *International Journal of Disability, Development and Education, 65*(2), 229–242. doi:10.1080/1034912X.2017.1368460

Naicker, L. (2013). The journey of South African women academics with a particular focus on women academics in theological education. *Studia Historiae Ecclesiasticae, 39*(suppl. 1).

Ndlovu-Gatsheni, S. J. (2016). The emergence and trajectories of struggles for an 'African university': The case of unfinished business of African epistemic decolonisation. *Kronos, 43*(1), 51–77.

Ndofirepi, A., & Cross, M. (2017). University knowledge for societal change in Africa: Unpacking critical debates. In M. Cross & A. Ndofirepi (Eds.), *Knowledge and change in African Universities* (Vol. 1, pp. 1–14). Sense Publishers.

Osha, S. (2011). Appraising Africa: Modernity, decolonisation, and globalisation. In L. Keita (Ed.), *Philosophy and African development: Theory and practice* (pp. 169–176). CODESRIA.

Rahnema, M. (2001). Science, universities a+nd subjugated knowledges: A "Third World" perspective. In R. Hayhoe & J. Pan (Eds.), *Knowledge across cultures: A contribution to dialogue among civilizations*. Comparative Education Research Centre, University of Hong Kong.

Ramose, M. B. (2003). I doubt, therefore African philosophy exists. *South African Journal of Philosophy, 22*(2), 113–127.

Serequeberhan, T. (2002). The critique of Eurocentrism and the practice of African philosophy. In P. H. Coetzee & A. P. J. Roux (Eds.), *Philosophy from Africa* (pp. 87–110). Oxford University Press.

wa Thiong'o, N. (1998). Decolonising the mind. *Diogenes, 46*(184), 101–104.

Wallerstein, I. (1974). *The modern world-system: Capitalist agriculture and the origins of the European world-economy in the sixteenth century*. Studies in Social Discontinuity. Academic Press.

Yenika-Agbaw, V. (2014). Black Cinderella: Multicultural literature and school curriculum. *Pedagogy, Culture & Society, 22*(2), 233–250.

2 Reflection on Disability (and) Educational Justice in Africa's Structurally Unjust Society During the COVID-19 Pandemic Lockdown

Africa's Structurally Unjust Society During Lockdown

Erasmus Masitera

Introduction

In what ways has the COVID-19 pandemic exposed students living with disability to educational injustice? In what ways does structural injustice contribute to disability educational injustice? These are the leading questions which I seek to respond to in this chapter.

Like many disasters that occur in many countries, the advent of COVID-19 has caught states unprepared in terms of dealing with the pandemic on the one hand and on the other upholding educational rights of disabled individuals. Attempts at curbing the spread of the disease, unprecedented measures such as lockdown that includes social distancing (involving physical distancing as well, travel and work restrictions, and only essential services functioning, all others limited or strictly controlled) have been introduced. Due to these restrictions, untold consequences have also been experienced, especially in countries that are structurally unjust; the effects have been dire for individuals living with disability (ILD). ILDs' well-being has been compromised and their rights overridden. It has been a double tragedy for ILDs: on the one hand they are confronted by impairments (physical, sensory and/or mental limitations) and on the other societal disablement in the form of lockdown regulations, coupled by inconsiderate governing systems that neglect ILDs' existential realities. This is in the form of government that fails to provide social support/services, abusive enforcement of regulations by security services, and exclusion in (social) education. The structural injustice and its role in the marginalisation of students living with disabilities is underexplored, especially during the COVID-19 pandemic; thus indirectly rejecting diversity, I will therefore give attention to this in this chapter.

ILDs are, in most cases, the most disadvantaged individuals in that they always have something lacking and always need the assistance of others in order for them to live meaningful lives (Mateta, 2020). Their disadvantage comes from exclusion, marginalisation, stigmatisation and often antagonising circumstances that dehumanise them such as neglect, rejection, exclusion,

DOI: 10.4324/9781003228233-2

expulsion, and extreme poverty (Benbo et al., 2011, pp. 689–690; Ngubane-Mokiwa, 2018). ILDs are confronted with unfair and unjust treatment which makes it difficult for them to integrate into societal processes (Benbow et al., 2014, p. 1048), yet they are expected to compete and live like non-disabled individuals in the presence of structural injustice. This is the case in educational systems; individuals are socialised or integrated into society through educational processes (Matsika, 2012; Plato, cited in Cooper & Hutchison, 1997), but social injustice manifests its ugly head in educational circles, especially in that some of ILDs' needs are disregarded (absence of specialised assistive technologies, both human and material resources[1]). In this regard, the right to access education (formal and epistemological) is hindered through the abdication of society and state's obligation of availing accessible and adaptable schools that provide enabling learning environments for ILDs. This is regardless of various calls and advocacy for inclusive education (Musengi et al., 2012; Terzi, 2008), equal access to education (Terzi, 2008, 2010) and social justice for ILDs (Walker, 2005; Walker & Unterhalter, 2017). The absence of supportive infrastructure necessitates ILDs malfunctioning, thus promoting marginalisation. This marginalisation is a major contributor to the delinking and detachment ILDs encounter. Through this chapter, I will focus on ways of linking and promoting ILDs to higher educational justice during pandemics, particularly the COVID-19 outbreak. This is missing in literature linked to education and disability studies.

With that in mind, I will first discuss what disability justice is and its relation to education. Second, I will examine structural injustice with regard to how structural injustice militates against the achievement of disability justice in light of educational rights. Third, I will discuss state (educational) obligations. Fourth, my focus will be on the COVID-19 pandemic measures or implications of the restrictions on disability and educational justice, especially increasing the exclusion of ILDs. Fifth, I will explore possible means of achieving disability justice in education in pandemics; this is a way of advocating for diversity and inclusion of ILDs. Sixth, will be the conclusion of the chapter.

Disability Justice in Education

Generally, justice refers to an ideal, an expected standard, a canon or yardstick for judging human conduct either as right or wrong (Braswell, 2015, p. 6; Kanu, 2015, p. 78). Importantly, justice implies the endeavour to achieve and or establish and formulate acceptable and appropriate relations that enhance human living. Justice in a sense speaks of human interactions such as relationships among citizens and relationships between citizens and state institutions. To this end, Kelsen (2000, p. 1) pronounces that "justice is [a]... quality of a social order regulating the mutual relations of men." Additionally, Scheffler (2007, p. 69) opines that "justice requires that each person be given the ... advantage that he or she deserves." A summation of the foregoing view on justice comes from Buchanan and Mathieu (1986, p. 11) who view justice

10 *Erasmus Masitera*

as an end product that persons receive and as that which individuals are entitled to that are the benefits and burdens owing to each person in regard to their particular characteristics and circumstances. As such, justice is concerned with duties and obligations that individuals have towards each other; it also talks of duties and obligations that individuals have towards social institutions and vice versa (Campbell, 2010, pp. 6–9; Moyo, 2015, p. 71).

With regard to the above, disability justice, like any other form of justice, is the search for a standard or a measure of human conduct on individuals or groups that live with disability or disabilities of various forms. In this sense disability justice is the examination of society's activities; the duties and obligations that individuals have towards each other (be it ILDs or not) and also the examination of social structures (personal and institutional) in either advancing and/or hindering the realisation of dignity for individuals living with disability.

The activities of society have mostly been examined through the rights discourses, distributive discourses, contractarian discourses, identity discourses, epistemic and relational (in)justice discourses, among others (cf. Putman et al., 2019). Keifer-Boyd et al. (2018, p. 268) put it differently by postulating that disability justice is presented in two ways. Firstly, it involves activism against entanglements and other forms of oppression of people with disability. Secondly, it is a framework of analysing oppression that ILDs face. Disability as activism and as a framework reveals that disability justice is both an ethical issue and a struggle for liberation. As an ethical issue, disability justice analyses and critiques various forms of disadvantaging ILDs such as exclusion, marginalisation, stigmatisation, powerlessness, vulnerability and dependence of individuals living with disabilities. As activism, disability justice seeks recognition, respect and inclusion for the same people. Disability justice is a call to dismantle hierarchies associated with oppression and exclusion of ILDs, and a search for collective emancipation through the establishment of an acceptable society where all live dignified lives, that is, realising their well-being. By well-being I mean the realisation of socio-politico-economic wellness (Kleist, 2010). This entails the removal of hindrances and the opening of opportunities for all; moreover, supported by a functional welfare system that supports and promotes disadvantaged individuals.

In light of that, I contextualise disability justice, especially the ILDs' rights to access higher education during the COVID-19 pandemic. Among other expectations, disability justice in higher education is that in order for learning and teaching to effectively occur, the state ought to intervene on the part of the disabled by providing for ILDs' needs such as learning aids in the form of technological assistive machines. These assist in bridging the gap that some ILDs have and thus reducing or equalising the teaching and learning environments. During pandemics such as the COVID-19 outbreak, assistive technology becomes a necessity for the ILDs as online teaching and learning has become the norm. Furthermore, there is a sense of inclusion, reducing exclusion and marginalisation, boosting self-esteem, image and participation on the part of ILDs. Disability justice recognises rights, and promotes and

Disability (and) Educational Justice During Lockdown   11

maintains the dignity of ILDs so that they participate and contribute meaningfully to both their own lives and that of their communities. I emphasise here that structurally unjust societies fail to fulfil the expectation of disability justice in higher education. I now turn my attention to structural injustice and its relation to (un)just education.

Understanding Structural Injustice

Structural injustice is the systematic deprivation of essentials that individuals in society need in order to live a dignified life (Young, 2006, p. 2). The deprived essentials that individuals encounter are in the form of rights, dignity and well-being. According to Young (2006, pp. 1–2) and Alkire (2008, pp. 1–2), structural injustice refers to limited access to amenities, especially amenities that are necessary for particular individuals or groups of people to attain standard (respectable) livelihoods, dignity and well-being. Deprivations are limitations which society can overcome. In other words, deprivation is human-caused since it is an error of commission and omission on the part of the community and state. The deprivations in most cases are an exhibition of deficiency in structural organisation or a deliberate neglect of what individuals ought to have. Young (2006, p. 3) avers that this deprivation is a result of a system and/or a social process that produces and reproduces inequalities. This may be in the form of lacking infrastructure or activities that marginalise other individuals in the state. There is therefore a sense in which opportunities and wellness and individual autonomy are infringed upon. However, the crux of the matter is that structural injustice is a lack in promoting dignity and well-being.

The limited realisation of well-being is a result of biased and other unfair decisions and practices in responding to situations (Alkire, 2008, p. 1). The same ideas are expressed by Eriksen (2017, p. 1) who opines that infringement of fundamental rights emanates from various state structures that support discrimination and exploitation. In the same vein, Parekh (2011, p. 676) avers that structural injustice unfairly constrains people's opportunities, while granting others privileges. The views expressed here raise a fundamental question as to whether social injustice is (always) intentional or unintentional. According to Young (1997), social injustice is unintentional in as much as social injustice is not caused by an individual and is an unconscious habitual action of several individuals; that social injustice is embedded in norms, habits and everyday actions; and that social injustice is not oppression as it is not "created" or caused. In not so direct confrontation of Young's thinking, Jugov and Ypi (2019, p. 3) aver that a structure is a social creation and hence implicates everyone associated with its creation, and maintenance or reproduction of (in)justice emanating from it. In that sense, social injustice is human-caused and human-created, and can be corrected by the same humans.

With regard to the foregoing view, one may think of the electoral campaigns that occur (in most African countries), where the campaigners promise good governance in all its forms yet when elected they tend to do the opposite. This implies that they are fully aware of what is right, yet deliberately choose to do the opposite. These sentiments are shared by Owen (2020, p. 2590), who argues that social structures are human creations. Based on Rawls's (1971) postulations, social structures are designed to: (i) create a fair distribution; (ii) prevent subsequent background injustices which could emerge without any individual acting wrongly. In this chapter, I share the views of Jugov and Ypi (2019), Rawls (1971) and those of Owen (2020) that implicate humans in directly causing and creating injustices, especially those that inhibit or constrain other individuals in realising their well-being.

In relation to the aims of this chapter, structural injustice is the underlying cause of social injustices connected to the failure of ILDs to access higher education and making that education adaptable to the requirements of a particular society. My argument is that individual (selfish) interests directly and indirectly cause individuals to establish institutions that benefit them and are impervious to the oppression of others. There is a sense in which social injustice is an abdication of moral (and political) responsibility to care, protect and promote each other's livelihood. According to Ndlovu-Gatsheni (2020), extractivism (as a form of social injustice) that is informed by colonial epistemologies is the cause and development of self-preservation among Africans and this is against the idea of African communal living and thinking. Extractivism is exhibited through self-enriching projects such as embezzlement of coffers, and corrupt activities. Consequently, the financing of state activities is affected and, in most cases, areas that require funding so as to sustain human life suffer the most.

Social injustice exhibits itself in social, political and economic realms. In all these realms, ILDs suffer more than any group of people. In relation to disability, structural injustice is revealed through social systems that are skewed or that favour the well-being of individuals who have no disability. There is an absence of social support systems that prioritise ILDs. ILDs are more often persistently and perpetually disadvantaged by social structures or systems of rules and practices that make the distribution of resources unfair, unequal and exclusionary. ILDs are expected to compete on an equal footing for opportunities and access to social goods as if they have equal talents and physical abilities as non-disabled beings; yet this is not the case. Further to that, social narratives also often neglect individuals living with disability. The absence of inclusive social structures and inclusive social practices that enable individuals living with disability to properly function often results in subtle exclusion and marginalisation of individuals living with disability(ies).

One may think of absence and non-affordability of assistive technologies or infrastructure that cater for individuals with disability, or think of lack of access to essential information as part of the exclusion process. Note that disability is not homogeneous; it is heterogeneous to such an extent that some individuals have multiple disabilities. Even then certain disabilities require specialised assistance for them to access essential information and services. Such services sometimes require communities to act together to promote and protect the dignity and well-being of everyone. For the ILDs this includes special or dedicated infrastructure, responsive or adaptive health care systems, responsive technological and social infrastructure, among others. However, in structurally unjust societies this is absent; as such the needs of the ILDs (that which they lack and that which requires provision from the community) are disregarded. The neglect of ILDs implies that there is a disregard for their rights and well-being; in educational matters it means they are excluded, and diversity is challenged. The blame for such neglect or rather abdication of duty lies in the state or government of the day. Note it is the duty of the state to protect, promote and advance the well-being of individuals through provision of safety nets (distribution funds and strategic provision of resources necessary) that advance dignity and well-being of people. However, the obligation is two-way: on the one hand individuals have to act through their agency to claim and demand what is due to them, and on the other hand the government has to be responsive positively and provide for that which is required by the citizens. It is the latter point that is of interest to this work, and which will be my focus. In that regard, I now turn to the obligations of the state and, in particular, provision of higher education to ILDs.

State Obligation and Duties in Education Rights

In order for individuals to realise their dignity, governments ought to protect, preserve and promote the lives of all citizens, irrespective of the individuals' backgrounds (Sen, 1999). Political philosophers and scientists classify this as part of the obligations and duties that governments have towards their citizens. The obligations and duties that governments have to fulfil are further stipulated in a state constitution, which draws inspiration from the Universal Declaration of Human Rights Charter of 1948 (UDHRC). The proclamations of the UDHRC range from political, social and economic facets of human living. However, the focus of this chapter is more on the social realm, in particular on educational rights. Educational rights are aptly expressed and elaborated upon by the United Nations Educational, Scientific and Cultural Organisation (UNESCO), which is a body that specialises in matters that have to do with education. In fact, the Zimbabwean state constitution, UDHRC and UNESCO all underscore that it is the responsibility of the state to advance the rights of citizens in matters of education.

According to UNESCO (2020) governments have a duty to make education available, accessible, acceptable and adaptable to the people within their geographical location. This expectation encourages governments to participate in the process of removing factors which hinder individuals from attaining basic education, and encourages governments to eliminate any form of underdevelopment linked to lack of access to education. Education is considered one of the ways through which individuals become enlightened and possibly change the world, more so with higher education. In this way, epistemic enlightenment and the broadening of horizons of individuals are possibly attained and may be used to critique, advocate and bring about individual

14 *Erasmus Masitera*

emancipation or change the world for the good of everyone. Further to the UNESCO expectations, state constitutions are meant to bind government and at the same time give citizens guidance on what they are to expect from the government. In most cases, citizens expect their rights (freedoms and livelihoods) to be honoured and upheld; that is, creating socio-economic-political environments that eradicate advantaged and disadvantaged positions for individuals in society by creating equal opportunities and catering for the needs of all. As such, there is a correlation between citizens' expectations and government duties; there is therefore a symbiotic relation in exchange of views between governments and citizens (interchange of services and demands). On the part of the citizens, government demands cooperation so as to achieve set goals, and on the part of the government, citizens expect protection, promotion and securing of life in addition to that which is stated above. Overtly and covertly, the services provided by government have effects on promoting freedoms and enhancing the lives/well-being of the citizens through guaranteeing opportunities and means for citizens to live lives they value. This is expected in educational matters. I will now make a specific reference to the Zimbabwean scenario.

In relation to promoting and providing educational rights to citizens, the Zimbabwean government has, among other things, committed itself to "take all practical measures to promote … higher and tertiary education" in addition to providing free primary education. Additionally, and connected to the ethos of this chapter, the Constitution of Zimbabwe (2013, Number 83) states that persons with disability are to be enabled to participate fully in the lives of their communities through inclusion based on non-exploitation and non-abuse, access to required treatment and infrastructure and, above all, access to state-funded education. In other words, by confirming these duties in writing, the government is promising to be responsible for promoting effective learning for all people regardless of abilities or inabilities.

However, due to economic challenges, the expectations have not been fulfilled. Economic challenges have led to the collapse of social services that most marginalised individuals need (healthcare, education, state sponsored social welfare, to mention a few). In fact, economic challenges have also destroyed safety nets that many citizens relied on. Implicitly, the government has neglected its duties and responsibilities as well by withdrawing or allocating inadequate resources to the education sector. Rather, the government has chosen to play a role of determining or advising only; for example, it determines opening and closing dates, graduation dates and controlling or determining the quality of education. Yet despite these roles, it neglects its own core duties, that is, funding education, ensuring that everyone can access education and even that the education be acceptable and adaptable to communities and in tandem with social circumstances (cf. Hill, 2014). Failure to provide safety nets and even stabilise the economy may be interpreted as an element of social injustice, that is, failure to protect individuals from conditions that expose them to distressing conditions. Furthermore, failure and neglect to protect and honour expectations hinders the right to access education as some may not be in a position to fund themselves, inadvertently leading to covert exclusion and, in the long run, discrimination and exclusion (cf. UNESCO, 2020) through infrastructures that are not adaptable to the needs of ILDs.

Yet the lack of state-funded social services increases vulnerability on the part of those who live on the margins of society, especially individuals living with disability. Peta and Moyo (2019, p. 87) suggest that, "[i]n every region of the world, persons with disability often live on the margins of society, deprived of the most basic human rights and fundamental freedoms"; the disadvantaged position is increased during disasters (natural disasters such as COVID-19 outbreak). On the one hand, there is a lack of social nets by the government and, on the other, social exclusion (discrimination, marginalisation, poverty, joblessness etc.) of various forms augment their disadvantaged position. Natural disasters such as disease outbreaks require immediate action and reactions to control or alleviate suffering on the part of the citizens, yet these activities require significant funding from the government and other related partners.

However, in underdeveloped economies such as Zimbabwe, there are severe constraints to this: either there are no funds at all set aside to cater for such unfortunate events and/or there is government unwillingness to commit itself to this. So natural disasters bring double jeopardy for individuals living with disability; social exclusion they already have as well as social or state inactivity to better their situation in difficult times. In terms of education, COVID-19 brought changes such as technological delivery methods; yet, due to poverty and lack of access to required technological equipment, individuals living with disability encounter further exclusion. In a sense there is structural injustice which contributes to educational exclusion and marginalisation of people with disability in periods of natural disasters. I now focus on how the COVID-19 lockdown contributed to disability injustice in higher education.

Lockdown, Structural Injustice, and Disability Injustice in Higher Education

On the level of higher education, ILDs encounter insurmountable difficulties. Lockdown demands social distancing and often this amounts to social and physical distancing. As Mateta (2020) observes, that COVID-19 has dealt a terrible blow to ILDs since most of them require human assistance. Such help includes physical contact, acquiring financial support, or assistive technologies. By saying this, Mateta highlights that disability is an area of need that requires social, economic, and political responses in the form of assistance.

However, due to different forms of impairments and social barriers impacted by the lockdowns, the disabled populations face double tragedy. On the one hand, social barriers make it difficult for them to operate freely and to realise a dignified livelihood. For instance physical distancing or social distancing is enforced, implying for most ILDs the absence of physical assistance which makes it difficult for them to operate. Yet again, having assistance from members of the society puts ILDs in danger of contracting the disease; think

16 *Erasmus Masitera*

of individuals who are visually impaired or who are wheelchair bound and getting assistance from members of the community who may be infected. However, in responsive and responsible communities people living with disability would normally be provided with or have access to assistive technologies so that they operate autonomously without requiring much human assistance. Provision of assistive technology would ensure protection of such individuals from contracting dangerous diseases. This is not the case with structurally unjust societies because, as stated before, in such communities there are limited, neglected or absent provision of amenities. In other words, there is a lack of responsibility on the part of the state. I raise this point to show the general challenge(s) that ILDs face in accessing needed amenities. This applies to educational circles and violates the educational rights of ILDs. Among other violated rights is the right to protection from social harm (living in a healthy environment), there is extended limited participation in the life of the institution to which one is affiliated (through failure to access institutional infrastructures and having no access to technology that enables participation).

In the case of higher education, the accessibility of academic facilities is reduced; for instance accessing entry into university itself, and entry into the library infrastructure (physical books, and internet services) is suspended. The suspension, due to the pandemic, impacts negatively on the expected learning outcomes, and there is also direct and indirect hindrance to accessing knowledge associated with enrolment and use of higher educational facilities. In this sense then, the academic well-being of IDLs is affected. Note that through education, one's self-esteem, self-actualisation, self-confidence, critical and analytical skills are enhanced, so through suspension of certain educational activities these expectations are unachieved. These are further inhibited through the absence of supportive systems which universities and the state could provide to the students and lecturers. Provisions such as data and availability of other teaching and learning materials are not supplied. This is reflective of unjust structures (dysfunctional and mismanaged, prioritised funding areas) state and institutional systems.

Injustice in higher education for ILDs leads to decreased epistemological formation as epistemological formation comes through access to epistemological facilities (educated individuals and libraries). By epistemological access I mean accessing various forms of knowledge that may be generated by higher education institutions. That is, developing individuals to be knowledgeable of a particular area and also to become critical and analytical individuals who participate and engage meaningfully in their communities (Ogone, 2017; Walker, 2019, p. 228). This view is derived from Morrow's (1994, p. 40) thinking which defines epistemological access as having a broader understanding of education beyond accessing educational institutions and infrastructure. Thus, formal access refers to accessing facilities as well as opportunities for personal growth and learning provided during the period of registration. In this case I note the importance of interaction among students, with university staff and the wider community that deal with the university. As such the interactions are important in shaping a student into a totally different individual, changing

Disability (and) Educational Justice During Lockdown   17

students' perception about community and the world at large. The interactions mean a lot and are pertinent in influencing behaviour and thinking as well. Yet with the advent of COVID-19 and the restrictions imposed, that learning process has been interrupted, thus hindering the growth which one ought to acquire. This view applies to both ILDs and those not disabled. However, more disruptions are faced by the disabled, some of whom require extra help from non-disabled members of the community, these members may choose to stay away for fear of contracting and spreading the disease.

In addition, other educational systems have not been spared this disruption. According to the United Nations (2020, p. 2), the interruptions brought by COVID-19 have affected "nearly 1.6 billion learners" worldwide and have also reduced "the opportunities... to continue learning." The disrupted learning outcomes and possible opportunities cut across educational levels that range from pre-primary levels, to primary, secondary, and tertiary institutions (United Nations, 2020, p. 7). Among the opportunities that education offers is the inculcation of values and, in the context of Africa, the dissemination of values such as community shared values suffer (not only is this a theoretical aspect but it is practically lived as well, the interactions and sharing living experiences). Thus, self-understanding and understanding of the community has been affected and/or hindered by the COVID-19 lockdown and social integration through interaction in class and beyond has been marred. By self-understanding I refer to the formation or realisation of one's being. My use of the term being in this case follows closely the Capability Approach understanding of the term, that is, the state, the kind of life that one may want to realise (Seon-Mi & Sharraden, 2014, p. 203). The idea of being is connected to the mental activity of choosing and acting within a given environment. Reflecting on ILDs and in a restricted environment (social distancing and structurally unjust societies) the being (choosing and acting) of such individuals is hindered by the fact that the assistance they need most is distanced from them. As part of "being" formation, education plays a pertinent role: it enlightens, guides, opens up opportunities and contributes significantly to building individuals and communities. Yet restriction and unjust systems restrict all this through limiting educational related interactions. Unjust societies generally increase the conditions of the marginalised through depriving ILDs of their needs and means of survival through absence of proper welfare support and other survival nets that would enable such people to live the kind of lives they would choose. In this case, structurally unjust societies enable the perpetuation of injustice.

Further to the injustice noted above, unjust systems also significantly contribute to the diminishing formation of being by underfunding educational activities. According to UNESCO, access and affordable education is a right (for higher education this is a human right), and one way this may be realised is through state funding. The funding would have assisted students in accessing much needed assistive technologies for ILDs and assistive communicative technologies through which educational materials and other forms of interaction would have been realised. As stated before, due to COVID-19 restrictions,

18   *Erasmus Masitera*

many countries have moved to online teaching and learning where the medium of communication is communicative technologies which include various forms of computers and smart phones. However, due to the expensive nature of technologies, not every individual is in a position to buy them and this is even worse for Zimbabweans whose economy is in a comatose state. Absence of social support that caters for health, education and other welfare factors for the marginalised of the community critically disempower people living with disability in that they are left exposed to limited educational opportunities. When the marginalised do not have opportunities to broaden their choices of living in a community/state, this also restricts their epistemological development.

In the foregoing discussion, there are implicit ideas of exclusion, marginalisation and discrimination on individuals living with disability. Exclusion comes through denial of access to that which one is entitled to through society's failure to provide for that which enhances or may cause one to realise their dream. In this case I am thinking of failure to access both infrastructure and epistemological outcomes. A disabled individual is denied this right through the social structures and socially imposed restrictions which do not consider the requirements, needs and well-being of ILDs. Discrimination is also concealed in the activities of the community, especially through the law which considers all individuals as equal, yet in reality individuals are different. The lockdown restrictions have no exceptions to cater for disabled individuals, the laws are applied to all individuals without exception. Think of individuals who have hearing impediments; in sign language, facial expression is essential. Masking up has been mandatory during the lockdown period; imagine how this has affected individuals who rely on facial reading in order to make sense of what is being said. Discrimination in this sense is in the forms of lack of access to vital information. Besides this, in the case of Zimbabwe, Mateta (2020) notes that most information is inaccessible to the disabled, especially the blind and deaf. He notes that only about 30% of individuals in this category are able to read and write (in braille) and 70% are unable to do both. This tacit discrimination against disabled individuals is thus rampant and generally not regarded in society and, in particular, structurally unjust societies. There has been no effort to better the position of individuals living with disability to access information and even change their livelihood. Evidently, the idea of inclusion and diversity in matters that have to do with education, and higher education in particular, has been neglected.

Recommendations on Enhancing Well-Being of ILDs

i. Proper representation. There is need to realise that disability is equal to other sectors of society such as the women or youth sectors who are represented at different levels of social living. A representative from among the ILD group would be vital as they are aware of the needs of individuals in that category. This becomes helpful especially when faced with natural disasters such as pandemics.

Disability (and) Educational Justice During Lockdown   19

ii.   Serious consultations with members living with disability. This should be done to increase participation and awareness of the needs of such individuals.

iii.   Encourage inclusive and genuine dialogue. Be honest and act upon the expectations of such individuals. This is connected to the previous point but different in that the emphasis is now on recognition and respect of such individuals.

iv.   Government must provide technical and moral support to improve the lives of ILDs. This will help protect them from the adverse effects of natural disasters and other pandemics. Welfare strategies should ensure that access to higher education is improved by providing digital gadgets and the funds to support higher education.

v.   Improved communication that is packaged in different formats that suits different disabilities.

Conclusion

In this article, I have argued for the improved role of the government in advancing educational justice for ILDs. I argue that provisions have to be provided for the disabled; this is mostly the role of the government. This is possible through serious engagement of the state and ILDs; however, communication has to be improved. Communication has to be inclusive and feedback from ILDs needs to be respected and acted upon. Furthermore, authentic representation of ILDs has to be enhanced. The enhanced interaction respects rights, strengthens dignity and the livelihoods of ILDs especially during pandemics when ILDs are likely to face double tragedies emanating from poor governance and from various forms of societal exclusions. I therefore identified education non-provision of ILDs' needs as a case in point in revealing the injustices that ILDs face, especially in unjust societies and during the COVID-19 pandemic. By arguing for rights, dignity and livelihoods for the ILDs, I propose a means by which transformed societies that are inclusive and that react to ILDs' needs may be achieved, and at the same time avoid further recurrence of injustice towards such individuals.

Note

1   These assist ILDs to comprehend and participate in educational processes.

References

Alkire, S. (2008). *Concepts and measures of agency. Oxford poverty and human development initiative* (Working Paper Series # 9).

Benbo, S., Forchuk, C., & Ray, S. (2011). Mothers with mental illness experiencing homelessness: A critical analysis. *Journal of Psychiatric and Mental Health Nursing, 18*(8), 687–695.

20 *Erasmus Masitera*

Benbow, S., Rudwick, A., Forchuk, C., & Edward, B. (2014). Using a capability approach to understand poverty and social exclusion of psychiatric survivors. *Disability and Society*, *29*(7), 1046–1060.

Braswell, M. C. (2015). Ethics, crime and justice: An introductory note to student. In M. C. Braswell, B. R. McCarthy & B. J. McCarthy (Eds.). *Justice, crime and ethics* (pp. 1–8). Routledge.

Buchanan, A., & Mathieu, D. (1986). Philosophy and justice. In R. L. Cohen (Ed.), *Justice: Views from the social sciences* (pp. 11–20). Plenum Press.

Campbell, T. (2010). *Justice*. Palgrave Macmillan.

Constitution of Zimbabwe Amendment (No. 20) Act, 2013 [Zimbabwe].

Cooper, J. M., & Hutchison, D. S. (Eds.). (1997). *Plato: Complete works*. Hackett Publishing Co.

Eriksen, E. O. (2017). Structural injustice: The European crises and the duty of solidarity. In A. Grimmel & S. M. Giang (Eds.), *Solidarity in the European Union* (pp. 97–118). Springer.

Hill, P. (2014). *Rethinking the state role in education*. crpe.org/thelens/rethinking-state-role-education

Jugov, T., & Ypi, L. (2019). Structural injustice, epistemic opacity and the responsibilities of the oppressed. *Journal of Social Psychology*, *50*(1), 7–27.

Kanu, A. M. (2015). A philosophical appraisal of John Rawls' Difference Principle in the context of the Quorta System of Nigeria. *Philosophy Study*, *5*(2), 78–85.

Keifer-Boyd, K., Bastos, F., Richardson, J., & Wexler, A. (2018). Disability justice: Rethinking "Inclusion" in arts education research. *Studies in Art Education A Journal of Issues and Research*, *59*(3), 267–271.

Kelsen, H. (2000). *What is justice? Justice, law and politics in the mirror of science*. The Lawbook.

Kleist, C. (2010). Global ethics: Capabilities approach. *Internet Encyclopedia of Philosophy: A Peer-Reviewed Academic Resource*. www.iep.utm.ed/ge-capb/

Mateta, A. (2020). Presentation, conversations on COVID-19 and human rights in Zimbabwe. 'COVID-19 and disability'. In *Inequality and the rights of disadvantaged groups*. Webinar presentation on 23 July 2020.

Matsika, C. (2012). *Traditional African education: Its significance to current educational practices with special reference to Zimbabwe*. Mambo Press.

Morrow, W. (1994). Entitlement and achievement in education. *Studies in Philosophy and Education*, *13*(1), 33–47. doi:10.1007/BF01074084

Moyo, K. (2015). Mimicry, transitional justice and the land question in racially divided former settler colonies. *The International Journal of Transitional Justice*, *9*(1), 70–89.

Musengi, M., Ndofirepi, A., & Shumba, A. (2012). Rethinking education of deaf children in Zimbabwe: Challenges and opportunities for teacher education. *Journal of Deaf Studies and Deaf Education*, *18*(1), 62–74.

Ndlovu-Gatsheni, S. (2020). The cognitive empire, politics of knowledge and Africa intellectual productions: Reflections on struggles for epistemic freedom and resurgence of decolonization in the twenty-first century. *Third World Quarterly*, 882–901. https://doi.org/10/1080/01436597.2020.1775487

Ngubane-Mokiwa, S. A. (2018). Ubuntu considered in light of exclusion of people with disabilities. *African Journal of Disability*, 7, 460. https://doi.org/10.4102/ajod.v7i0.460

Ogone, J. O. (2017). Epistemic injustice: African knowledge and scholarship in the global context. *Postcolonial Justice*, 17–36. https://doi.org/10.1163/9789004335196_004

Disability (and) Educational Justice During Lockdown 21

Owen, D. (2020). Migration, structural injustice and domination on 'Race' mobility and transnational positional differences. *Journal of Ethnic and Migration Studies, 46*(12), 2585–2601.

Parekh, S. (2011). Getting to the root of gender inequality: Structural injustice and political responsibility. *Hypatia, 26*(4), 672–689.

Peta, C., & Moyo, A. (2019). The rights of persons with disabilities in Zimbabwe. In A. Moyo (Ed.), *Selected aspects of the 2013 Zimbabwean Constitution and the Declaration of Rights* (pp. 86–125). Raoul Wallenberg Institute of Human Rights and Humanitarian Law.

Putman, D., Wasserman, D., Blustein, J., & Asch, A. (2019). Disability and justice. *Stanford Encyclopedia of Philosophy*, viewed 18 February 2020, from plato.stanford.edu/entries/disability-justice/

Rawls, J. (1971). *A theory of justice*. The Belknap Press.

Scheffler, S. (2007). Distributive justice and economic desert. In S. Olsaretti (Ed.), *Desert and justice* (pp. 69–92). Clarendon Press.

Sen, A. (1999). *Development as freedom*. Oxford University Press.

Seon-Mi, K., & Sharraden, M. S. (2014). The capability approach and social justice. In M. Reisch (Ed.), *Routledge international handbook of social Justice*. https://doi.org/10.4324/9781315857534

Terzi, L. (2008). *Justice and equality in education: A capability perspective in disability and special education needs*. Bloomsbury Publishing.

Terzi, L. (2010). What metric of justice for disabled people? In H. Brighouse & I. Robeyns (Eds.), *Measuring justice: Primary goods and capabilities* (pp. 150–173). Cambridge University Press.

United Nations. (2020). *Education during COVID-19 and beyond*.

United Nations Educational, Scientific and Cultural Organisation (UNESCO). (2020). *Right to education: State obligations and responsibilities*. https://en.unesco.org/themes/right-to-education/state-obligations

Walker, M. (2005). Amartya Sen's capability approach and education. *Educational Action Research, 13*(1), 103–110.

Walker, M. (2019). Defending the need for a foundational epistemic capability in education. *Journal of Human Development and Capabilities, 20*(2), 218–232. https://doi.org/10.1080/19452829.2018.1536695

Walker, M., & Unterhalter E. (2017). *Amartya Sen's capability approach and social justice in education*. Palgrave Macmillan.

Young, I. M. (1997). *Intersecting voices: Dilemmas of gender, political philosophy, and policy*. Princeton University Press.

Young, I. M. (2006). Responsibility and global justice: A social connection model. *Social Philosophy and Policy, 23*(1), 102–130.

3 Improving Processes, Practices and Structures in South African Higher Education
Voices of Students with Disabilities

Sibonokuhle Ndlovu

Introduction

Students with disabilities have been denied to be knowledge contributors to education by virtue of their continual exclusion in South African higher education. Though there has largely been increased access into higher education (Howell, 2006), entry into professional programmes, and learning particularly, are still limited for the particular students because of inequitable processes, practices and structures (Ndlovu, 2017). More so, the design and structures of some professional programmes in themselves are limiting to students with disabilities. Odendaal-Magwaza and Farman (1997) have argued that some programmes have courses that involve field practice off-campus, use particular types of equipment, or require extensive interaction with the public. It is believed that students with disabilities themselves are also unable to meet some course demands due to their impairments (Odendaal-Magwaza & Farman, 1997). The Education programme is no exception to such limitations. Students with profound disabilities could be limited in using some equipment and extensive interaction is required. In essence, the particular students could be limited access into the programme right at entry. The exclusion at entry and in learning therefore makes them limited in contributing to professional knowledge, broadly, and Education specifically.

While extensive research has been conducted in terms of exclusion of students with disabilities in different programmes in South African higher education, this chapter's uniqueness is that it specifically focuses on students with disabilities' voice for their inclusion, specifically in the programme of Education. Professional knowledge in Education in particular is of interest in the context of South African higher education because of its history. During apartheid, Education was offered in teachers' colleges, and emphasis was placed on the practical rather than the theoretical aspect of knowledge (Welch, 2002). The post-apartheid era then saw teacher education being moved from teachers' colleges, which offered low-level content knowledge, to the higher education sector, which emphasises educational theoretical knowledge (Rusznyak, 2015). As for students with disabilities, it was not expected that they could attain professional knowledge in Education at higher education level. This

DOI: 10.4324/9781003228233-3

was because of the segregated education system that there was during apartheid, in which those with disabilities were placed in special schools, with a "toned down" curriculum.

The argument in this chapter is that the voice of students with disabilities themselves, who have a lived experience of disability, can improve the way they are included in the programme of Education, consequently making them contributors to the professional knowledge in Education at a level of higher education. This is because they know exactly how they should be taught in order to attain professional knowledge. Of importance is that the responsible authorities hear their voice and the suggested recommendations are implemented. Based on this argument, the particular students' voice therefore becomes of paramount importance to the improvement of their entry, learning and unique accommodations, that they could also consequently contribute to knowledge production in the field of Education and disability.

The chapter starts by discussing what constitutes professional knowledge in higher education generally, and the professional knowledge of Education in particular, which is the focus of the chapter. The methodology then describes the way in which the empirical study was carried out and the voices of students with disabilities on improving entry into the programme of Education, classroom teaching and accommodations relating to infrastructure at the school, are presented. The tool of coloniality of being, drawn from the broad decolonial theory, is used to illuminate the realities at entry, classroom teaching and the built environment, and invisible underlying causes. Possibilities of the students with disabilities' voice for improving their inclusion, and to acquire professional knowledge is then analysed. The conclusion is that only if the recommendations provided are listened to and implemented, will the voices have a positive influence.

Professional Knowledge in Higher Education

Defining professional knowledge, Dickson (2007) stated that it is know-about and know-how knowledge that is applied to practice. Thus, it is specialised knowledge of a specific profession (theoretical) and its practical application. There are elements of professional knowledge that are general across all programmes, and specialised knowledge that is specific to a particular profession. For example, in Law there is general professional knowledge for all law students and different specialised knowledge for advocates, attorneys, judicial and legal advisors. Abbott (1988), in agreement with Macdonald (1995), argued that professional knowledge is applied differently from one case to another, meaning that the theoretical and practical knowledge in a particular programme may not be applied the same way across the board. There is need for application of judgement on the part of a professional, implying that judgement is part of those important requirements that constitute professional knowledge. This was confirmed when Shalem (2014) explained that

24 *Sibonokuhle Ndlovu*

such judgement is expertise in decision-making that is also derived from theoretical knowledge. In relation to judgement in Education she argued that:

> Teachers have to exercise professional judgement when selecting emphasis for the content to be taught, designing a sequence of contents in a specific topic, choosing correct examples to demonstrate a concept, interpreting learners' errors, dealing with cultural differences in learners and so forth.
>
> (p. 7)

The above implies that professional judgement is an important aspect of professional knowledge because in order for a practitioner to contextualise and apply knowledge differently, as required by specific situations, professional judgement needs to be exercised (Shalem, 2014). Professional judgement and its application in practice is informed by a theoretical foundation of knowledge, and as Bigge and Shermis (1999) contended, one needs to be metacognitive about one's practice.

What constitutes professional knowledge differs from one professional degree programme to the next. In essence, each profession is defined by its autonomy. This implies that each programme is unique and has specialised knowledge that forms its foundation. This knowledge is different from each other, and makes one profession distinct from another and unique (Abbott, 1988). Haralambos and Holborn (1991) argued that there are high- and low-level professions. In the same tone, Young and Muller (2014) maintained that there are professions and semi-professions. What this implies is that there is also powerful and less-powerful professional knowledge, in line with professions and semi-professions. Medicine and Law, for example, fall into the category of high-level professions (Haralambos & Holborn, 1991), and are thus constituted by powerful professional knowledge (Young & Muller, 2013).

While professional knowledge for each programme is different, there are aspects that are common across all of them. Ethical standards specifically are emphasised as part of all professional practice (Higgs-Kleyn & Kapelianis, 1999). There is need for those who offer a specific professional programme to register with the respective professional body so that there is commitment to an ethical standard of practice. Proficiency in English is another requisite across all professional programmes. This is because students should be able to engage with and comprehend a standard interpretation of what their job entails, and be able to converse with all people through the international language. Furthermore, numeracy is also required for calculation. In this changing world, with rapid developments in technology, integrating technology to professional knowledge has also become key across all professions, implying that teaching and learning should now include technology. Students with disabilities also have to meet the same requirements for professionalisation as all other students. This is because they are also expected to produce knowledge, like all other graduates.

At one time, debates had raged about whether Education was a profession or a semi-profession (Hargreaves, 2000), which is a key requirement in the definition of a profession. The argument was that teachers were restricted because their practice was shaped, directed and monitored through organisational goals (Demirkasimoglu, 2010). In essence what it meant was that teachers' practice was controlled and their decision-making was restricted as they had to conform to a pre-designed curriculum, mandated by the state, to meet its ideology. Although they had a choice of teaching methods, they had to abide by specified standards and performance levels, which were regulated through public examinations. However, despite the external controls within which Education as a programme operates, Taylor and Runté (1995) argued that it is still a profession. In the South African context, the professional knowledge of Education has been developed since the apartheid period, to the extent that the programme of Education now qualifies as a profession. This is because professional theoretical knowledge is now embraced (Rusznyak, 2015), whereas it was not emphasised before. This implies that it now has its specialised knowledge on which it is founded, making it unique and different from all other professions.

Professional Knowledge in Education

What constitutes professional knowledge in a programme is generally broad. For Education, there are key elements and domains that constitute its professional knowledge. Internationally, scholars like Shulman (1986) and Badge (2014) have managed to provide specific knowledge tribes that constitute knowledge for Education. In the South African context, a number of scholars in the Education field, such as Clarke and Winch (2004), Shay (2013), Winch (2014), Shalem (2014), and Rusznyak (2015), have discussed what constitutes professional knowledge, both in primary and secondary sectors. In South Africa there are five basic professional knowledges a student should acquire in the field of Education. The Department of Higher Education and Training (as summarised in Table 3.1) classifies the types of knowledge found in the Education programme.

Table 3.1 Summary of the basic professional knowledge in education

Professional knowledge	Area of focus
Disciplinary/Subject Matter Knowledge	Foundational knowledge in Education and specialised knowledge of specific discipline.
Pedagogical Knowledge	Principles, practices and methods of teaching. Knowledge of learners and the curriculum.
Situational Knowledge	Learning about the South African context, knowledge of diverse learners and challenges they face.
Fundamental Knowledge	Learning to converse in second official language, Information and Communication Technologies.
Practical Knowledge	Study of practice and actual practising in classroom contexts.

Source: Adapted from the Department of Higher Education and Training (2015).

26 *Sibonokuhle Ndlovu*

All the knowledges put together in the above table constitute the professional knowledge of Education. As already highlighted regarding the components of all professional knowledge, in different programmes there is both theoretical and practical knowledge. Education is no exception; its practical knowledge involves learning from practice (Department of Higher Education and Training [DHET], 2015). As explained by Winch (2014), practical knowledge used to inform practice is, in turn, drawn from theoretical knowledge. Thus, both theoretical and practical knowledge need to be acquired by all students, including those with disabilities, if they are to graduate and make a contribution to knowledge production and its development in the spaces of higher education. When they are fully included in their learning, students with disabilities may also add different dimensions to knowledge production in Education, from the perspective of disability, as they have a lived experience of it. Their voice on how their inclusion could be improved is thus imperative. In the present chapter, their voice is presented and discussed as it relates to learning of theoretical knowledge in an institution of higher education, before acquisition of practical knowledge, in integrated learning settings (the workplace, as in schools).

Methodology

The empirical study had a qualitative research design, carried out with students with disabilities at an institution of higher education in South Africa. Sampling of participants was purposive (De Vaus, 1986), for a sample unit with particular features, which would enable detailed exploration, and yielding of rich data. In this study, the feature that was important concerned students who had a lived experience of studying professional knowledge in Education specifically, by virtue of studying the professional degree. Seven students with disabilities studying Education were selected through the snowballing technique (De Vaus, 1986). This means that participants assisted in finding other relevant participants. The participants, who were of different races, gender, ages and schooling background, were included in the sample, resulting in the attainment of maximum variation.

Data collection was qualitative, with data collected through in-depth unstructured individual interviews. They were preferred because, as Gubrium and Holstein (2001) have argued, they offer more flexibility. The interviews were conducted on a one-to-one basis, using a semi-structured interview guide. They took place at one formerly advantaged institution of higher education, with a Disability Unit (DU) anecdotally regarded as one of the best units in the country, associated with the institution (Ndlovu, 2017). All participants were interviewed in English because it was a common language understood by the interviewer and all participants. There were no communication barriers between the interviewer and participants with hearing impairments because all of them used oral communication.

Data were analysed thematically (Creswell, 2008; Leedy, 1997) and cross-checking of data was done, which Ndhlovu (2014) referred to as constant comparative analysis. It helped to identify contradictions and consistencies in the data. Responses from students with disabilities in terms of their voice were compared to each other. This was important for understanding intersectionality among students with disabilities as a factor in shaping their experience of professional learning. Finally, triangulation (Carter et al., 2014) was used to validate data from students in the programme. The study followed strict ethical considerations because of the vulnerability of students with disabilities. The ethics committee (clearance number 2013CE106D) granted ethics clearance. Permission to conduct the study was obtained from the institution and informed consent was sought from individual students with disabilities who volunteered to participate.

Voices on Equalisation of Opportunities in Entering Education

Students with disabilities were aware that the particular institution did not equalise opportunities of entry into the programme of Education, resulting in them being disadvantaged in accessing the programme. This was because the institution required the same entry-level requirements from all students, with or without disabilities. It was confirmed from such statements as reported below:

> I did not experience any problems myself to enter into Education because I had the entry requirements they needed. I did not struggle to get in. I had all the subjects and the points and so it was easy for me to enter.
>
> (Student Three)

The above statement suggests that students with disabilities are as academically able as all other students; they also meet the entry-level requirements, which make access possible without difficulties. However, this could not be generalised to all students with disabilities, because a greater number of students had a different view on equalisation of entry. Five of the seven participants stated that when opportunities of equalisation were not made, it was difficult for students with disabilities to enter into the Education programme. They said that, unlike able-bodied students, they were already disadvantaged from the level of schooling; as a result the playing field was not even for them. They echoed the voice that said:

> I want them to make special consideration in entry requirements and admissions because you can't pretend you don't have a disability.
>
> (Student Seven)

The statement above suggests that students with disabilities feel that they are unequal to other students, not in their academic capabilities, but in terms of opportunities, which are not equal at entry. The students' voice on equalising opportunities of access in entering Education draws attention to how the issue of equality is addressed in South African higher education in general. In Riddel et al. (2005), equality involves treating everyone in the same way. The first student's words seem to suggest that equality is viewed in terms of

28 *Sibonokuhle Ndlovu*

being treated the same way as other students. However, equality could be viewed as a controversial issue when understood as treating all people in the same way (Riddel et al., 2005) when they are different. It becomes a complex issue when an equal approach to people who are diverse and different discriminates against those who are already disadvantaged, and is a process that is used at entry at this particular institution. Equality can only be "equality" in a totally transformed and inclusive environment where all people in their diversities can access what they need at the time that they need it and are able to fully participate (Simons & Masschelein, 2005). The second statement implies that they think there could be better opportunities for their entry into the specific programme if their entry requirements could be considered differently and their limitations taken into account at the point of entry.

Coloniality of being would explain the exclusion of students with disabilities from entering the programme of Education as denial of difference, plurality and multiplicity by the dominant society. Ndlovu-Gatsheni (2001) maintained that through using normalcy as the standard measure, everyone has to be "normal". The entry requirements expected from all students with and without disabilities show that the limitations, setbacks and disadvantages of those with disabilities are not considered, setting a playing field that is disadvantageous for those students with disabilities. Their voice for consideration of special concession in terms of entry requirements could be seen as justified and relevant.

Students' Voices to Improve the Teaching Practice

The participants agreed that teaching at the institution required improvement in order for students with disabilities to access professional learning. Seven students with disabilities in the Education programme all agreed that the practice of teaching should be transformed to be inclusive of students with disabilities. The students stated that the fight should be on changing the mindset of the academic staff, who saw the students as a burden, hence their exclusion. They further stated that as students with disabilities, their voice was that the management should set a standard of teaching that is inclusive to all students, and establish measures that would ensure the unwilling academic staff adhered to established regulations. One of the students commented:

> If you are going to say the institution is inclusive and allow the person to work here, set the requirements for that person so that he practises inclusion! When you are lecturer with a disabled student in class, this and that is expected of you.
>
> (Student Two)

Another voice echoed the above when a student said that:

> What needs to change is the mindset of people. When it is not transformed, students with disabilities will still experience problems that would lead them to drop out before they finish the degree.
>
> (Student One)

Improving Processes, Practices and Structures 29

Across all statements, the common trend was that inclusion of students with disabilities in teaching of the knowledge of Education in higher education should be demanded and not negotiated, because without this, they would not complete their study. Their perception was that the university authorities should make specific ways to make the academic staff include students with disabilities and that they themselves should fight for this right. Such active engagement is an issue of self-advocacy. The voice of students with disabilities was confirmed in a study by Swart and Greyling (2011) in which students with disabilities also viewed self-advocacy as another way in which students themselves force inclusion by demanding from those who should provide it; and those in power as management, should use their power to enforce inclusion on the academic staff.

The students understood that the unwillingness of the academic staff could be the result of ignorance about how to teach students with disabilities. All seven students agreed that their exclusion from teaching might not be deliberate. Their voice was that they should help lecturers' ignorance by discussing how they should be taught.

> We should just get to a point where we actually start discussing it, we discuss the realities of the students living with a disability at the institution and lecturers are expected to understand and partake in such discussions.
>
> (Student Four)

They stated that it was the students with disabilities themselves who had to initiate these conversations and tell the particular lecturers of their disabilities. Ignorance in teaching students with disabilities has been echoed by a number of scholars (Matshedisho, 2007, 2010; Mutanga, 2017) and the reason underlying this was that the academic staff were not trained to teach this category of students (Mutanga, 2017). The students with disabilities' voice that open discussions with the lecturers who are ignorant about their unique learning needs was the way to overcome the challenge of ignorance, could be seen as appropriate. It can, in the time being fill the gap for lack of training on the part of academics.

Open discussions with lecturers also speak to the issue of disclosure of disabilities and openness to the lecturers, because some lecturers might not even be aware that there were such students in their class, especially those with invisible disabilities. Thus, the students with disabilities wanting to meet the lecturers half way, because they have realised their exclusion is unintentional, could be another way of also helping disclosure of disabilities, which some students find difficult to do. Creating awareness through talk is thus seen as a way that could drive change. With the students themselves initiating the talks, this can be seen as persons with disabilities having an opportunity to speak out to be heard. Hosking (2008) contended that the voice of those with disabilities is traditionally suppressed and marginalised. This is because those without disabilities always plan and speak on their behalf. So in an instance when the talk and discussion has been initiated by the students with disabilities themselves, power could be automatically transferred to them, and they might win.

30 *Sibonokuhle Ndlovu*

Coloniality of being further explains the invisible underlying cause of students with disabilities' exclusion from teaching. The teaching practice is designed and modelled around a "normal" student; in the process those who deviate from a "normal body and mind" as a set standard, are constructed as the other (Quijano, 2000). They are consequently left out by being the other. The teaching methods and the learning media used are for the normal. The time allocated for teaching and learning is for the "normal student". This could be seen as one way in which inequalities are perpetuated within coloniality in South African higher education. The coloniality of being therefore exposes how inequality emerges, resulting in students with disabilities' exclusion in teaching specifically. The voice seeking to counteract this "hidden" segregation is thus important.

Voice on Improving Built Environment

Students with disabilities in Education had experiences in which they were almost prevented from entering into the programme altogether because of physical structures at the specific university school. They stated that though they had the required entry requirements, with an inaccessible physical environment, their movements were restricted and, consequently, their access to learning venues. That this compounded to limit their access to learning and acquisition of professional knowledge, need not be overemphasised. The inaccessibility of the physical structures was confirmed in the statements below:

> When I was offered space to come and study Education, I thought it was because I had specified that I am on wheelchair and since they responded, the environment was conducive. To my biggest surprise, I found that the campus was almost inaccessible.
>
> (Student Seven)

At the specific School of Education, physical structures could have been more inaccessible as a result of history about those with disabilities and the education system in the South African context during apartheid. The segregation of education influenced even the infrastructure. It might not have been imagined that students with physical or visual disabilities from special schools could come to university in order to be professionalised in Education. It could be argued that the history of segregation in the country had negatively impacted the geography or physical landscape of the institution, specifically a portion of the campus in which the Education programme is conducted.

Evidence of this is reflected in the following student's statement:

> I understood because that campus, you know, with the field of Education in the country, it has never happened that a person on a wheelchair qualifies, so it was specifically for the able-bodied.
>
> (Student Five)

Improving Processes, Practices and Structures   31

The statement seems to suggest that the students with disabilities were aware of how a negative approach to disability could have influenced structures, and resulted in the physical inaccessibility at a particular school at the institution. Another one openly remarked:

> This campus was actually built during the apartheid era and no person with disabilities, no Black person, no Blacks were allowed into this campus ever!
>
> (Student Six)

The students' statements reveal that they were aware of the impact of apartheid on the accessibility challenges they confronted in terms of built environment at a particular school at the institution, and it was important that they give a voice that could enable their inclusion in terms of inaccessible infrastructure.

Students with disabilities in Education's voice on improving the built environment leaned towards individual accommodation. They recommended that instead of directing funding to improving buildings, it should be directed to meet the unique needs of individual students with disabilities. They saw this as a way in which they could be enabled access to professional learning for that particular time. Their argument was that it was not all students with disabilities' learning that was limited by the built environment. They stated that some were hindered by their specific impairments, and improving buildings would not be of much help to them. The reason for their voicing of individual accommodation could be understood from one student with physical disabilities who stated that she watched helplessly as renovations took place on old buildings in her school. The renovations did not help her get to the lecture venue to learn. She stated:

> While I was grounded with my broken wheelchair, I was asking myself, how is this construction going on here helping me to go and learn? Maybe they should have started by repairing my wheelchair!
>
> (Student Two)

Another one said:

> I think everyone who is disabled has specific needs; improving lecture theatres will not help us. We need things that are more direct to us.
>
> (Student One)

The students' voice for inaccessible built environment at their school was that they could be renovated or retrofitted, but not to the detriment or at the expense of individual students' needs. To them what mattered was meeting the individual needs so that they could access their professional learning first.

The particular students' concern was not only in the built environment generally but also in the seating places within the new learning venues, which were said to be built with disability in mind. According to the students, the

32 Sibonokuhle Ndlovu

seating places were also inaccessible and uncomfortable for their learning in the new buildings. Students with disabilities have ideas on how seating places inside the new learning venues could be improved. They thus recommended the improvement of the seating arrangements available for students using wheelchairs who were at that time limited by furniture because tables and chairs were on the stairs. Five of the seven students recommended that tables and chairs, which were connected to each other, be disconnected. They stated that this would create space and enable students with physical disabilities to move the chairs and tables and ensure their own comfort. They also suggested that innovations could be done on the chairs and tables themselves. One of the recommendations was:

> Something that could act as a table should be clipped on the side of the wheelchair. The student can then sit on his or her wheelchair and use that kind of a thing to write on anywhere.
>
> (Student Three)

The statement above reveals that students with disabilities are cognisant of what could be done if those with physical disabilities, specifically, had an input in the new seating arrangements in new structures.

Decolonial theory would point out the inaccessibility of the built environment largely as resulting from the general organisation of structures in society using "normalcy" as the standard (Quijano, 2000) and lack of consultation with the "other". As a result of this organisation, both social and physical structures were originally constructed and developed for what has also been constructed as the normal person. It is thus expected that the physical structures, more especially at the School of Education within the specific institution, be inaccessible. This has had a negative effect on students with disabilities, more specifically those with physical disabilities, those in wheelchairs and those with total visual loss. Inaccessibility of seating places in new buildings, said to be constructed with disability in mind, could also be explained by coloniality of being, as hierarchisation of people that results from categorising them, with people with disabilities ranking lower than those without disabilities (Ndlovu-Gatsheni, 2012). Thus, those without disabilities think, speak and do things for the "disabled", denying them their humanity. The exclusion persisting even in seating places in new buildings suggests that the students with disabilities were not consulted when the new buildings were constructed. The South African government is making every effort to address the inequalities of the past and segregative tendencies at different levels, and measures are more pronounced in higher learning (Ndlovu-Gatsheni, 2013). However, it has been revealed that the built environment is still inaccessible, even the new physical structures are also limited in terms of seating placement, all compounding to limit the professional learning of students with disabilities. Suggestions provided by students with disabilities are thus important as they could assist the responsible authorities to revisit what they have missed, even with new structures they are still constructing.

Possibilities of the Voices of Students with Disabilities

Possibility of Improving Entry into Education

An idea proposed by the students themselves, that their required entry points could be lowered because they are already disadvantaged from schooling, could be a way in which the inequitable structures and practices could be overcome. Special concession for entry-level requirements could indeed widen the opportunities of entry into Education for many students with disabilities, more particularly those from special schools. However, special concession for the particular student's entry into Education could be possible when the institution itself considers the idea and implements it. However, for an institution that is formerly advantaged and has high entry level requirements, there is a greater chance that making a special concession for other social groups of students might be viewed as lowering the academic standards. On the part of students with disabilities themselves, it could also exacerbate the low expectation of their intellectual capabilities, and consequently their performance, by the academic staff. This could result in the particular students being more oppressed in their learning than was happening before. Howell (2006) has argued that the academic staff in South African higher education have low expectations of students with disabilities' capabilities in general. Thus, while on one hand special concession at entry into education could assist students with disabilities gain access, on the other hand it could perpetuate the discrimination that occurred during apartheid, that those students were not capable for higher education generally, and the field of Education in particular.

Possibility for Improvement in the Practice of Teaching

The proposal of self-advocacy in which students with disabilities themselves negotiate with the academic staff on how to teach them, has a possibility for improving their inclusion in teaching. Swart and Greyling's (2011) study researched the self-advocacy of those with disabilities in South African higher learning and found that many students with disabilities are aware that they are the ones who should advocate for changing their circumstances, as no one else will do it for them. However, successful self-advocating requires specific skills and attributes, which students with disabilities should have developed. Getzel and Thoma (2008) have argued that for individuals with disabilities, knowledge of themselves, of their rights, communication skills, and problem-solving skills are important for self-advocacy. Furthermore, Swart and Greyling (2011) listed personal characteristics like patience, friendliness, determination and agency as necessary for students with disabilities who wish to self-advocate. Test et al. (2005) maintained that individuals with disabilities can develop self-advocacy independently, or it can be taught in the context of formal learning. Thus, the possibility of improving the teaching practice at the institution would depend on how students with disabilities

34 *Sibonokuhle Ndlovu*

self-advocate, as informed by the skills and knowledge of self-advocacy they have developed themselves.

The students' proposition that university authorities should resort to authoritative power to coercively force the academic staff to include them in teaching, might indeed improve their inclusion in classroom teaching at the particular institution. Such a proposition suggests that students with disabilities understand power as an authoritarian concept, a repressive thing possessed by particular social groups, classes or authorities in an institution who "reign it over and down upon others" (Tremain, 2005, p. 9). When power and authority are used that way, the university authorities could use it to enforce compliance of the academic staff as subordinates. When the lecturers comply, it may work favourably for the inclusion of students with disabilities in teaching. However, the kind of proposition in which university authorities can use power to coerce lecturers has its limitations. Foucault (1982) argued that use of power and authority works best when exercised to enable subjects and not to constrain them. What this implies is that power can work effectively when used persuasively and not coercively. Thus, use of power and cohesion might not yield the expected results, more especially within the democratic system in which higher education is located in South Africa. As the practice of teaching by the academic staff is central for the acquisition of professional knowledge in Education by students with disabilities, it is important that recommendations provided do not defeat the purpose for which they are made. It must not be glossed over again that the institution itself is a research-intensive university according to the categorisation of institutions in South Africa by the Council on Higher Education. This implies that more attention is directed to research than classroom teaching, more especially teaching undergraduate students. Students with disabilities, whose teaching requires an extra mile, might be more disadvantaged despite their voice for improving their inclusion in teaching.

Possibility for Improvement of the Physical Structures

The voice by students with disabilities that the authorities should direct intervention on their unique needs before they could make the physical structures accessible, has a possibility for their inclusion in professional learning. Swartz and Schneider (2006) reported that retrofitting existing buildings so that they are accessible to all, is challenging, expensive and amounts to a pipe dream in South Africa. This implies that even in the context of higher education, it may take a long time for the built environment to be accessible to all diverse students, including those with disabilities. Identifying individual needs and providing unique disability support or services to individual students with disabilities could be useful for the time before the built environment at the School of Education can be fully retrofitted or constructed for the accessibility to all diverse students, including those with disabilities. For example, repairing the wheelchair that has broken down for the student with physical disabilities, could assist the student get to the learning venues and acquire

Improving Processes, Practices and Structures 35

professional knowledge in Education at that particular time. Thus, before the attainment of full accessibility of the built environment for all students and those with disabilities—which may not happen soon—individual intervention or accommodation directed to individual students with disabilities could help their learning.

The recommendations provided by students with disabilities for adjusting the seating places could make it possible for the learning of professional knowledge by the particular student group. Fitchett (2015) reported that there was a lot of construction of new buildings which considered disability, and a lot of retrofitting was taking place at the specific institution, and this massive project had started at the particular School of Education. It was within such a context that seating places were still inaccessible to students with physical disabilities in wheelchairs. If the students in wheelchairs themselves have provided a way in which adjustments could be made, it could indeed help their learning, because they speak from the lived experience of disability (Devlin & Pothier, 2006). It would be most beneficial for the authorities and those involved with the particular students, such as the Disability Unit staff members, could listen to their voice. Hosking (2008) argued that by virtue of lived experience, those with disabilities' voice should be listened to. At times, those in power do not listen to the voice of those with disabilities. Titchkosky (2003) explained that when persons with disabilities say what the able-bodied want to hear, they are listened to, but when they say what those without disabilities do not want to hear, their voice is interpreted as an inappropriate response to disability. Against this background, the possibility that the voice of students with disabilities will be considered with regard to providing individual intervention or accommodation, and adjusting seating places, will depend on the willingness of those in power to listen and implement their recommendations.

Conclusion

The students with disabilities' voice on improving entry into Education, their inclusion in teaching and individual accommodation before improving infrastructure, is very important if they are to be professionalised like all other students. When they become included and consequently professionalised, there is a greater chance that they could also contribute to knowledge production in higher education. Their contribution to knowledge could bring another dimension, which is influenced by a lived experience of disability. It is therefore important that their voice be listened to, as they know exactly how their unique needs should be catered for, and how they should be involved in all that concerns them.

The voice of students with disabilities, which leans towards individual accommodation, has the possibility of enhancing professional learning but could be time-bound. A total transformation of the process of entry into Education, the practice of teaching and the built environment could have a lasting possibility for their acquisition of professional knowledge. Their voice

36 Sibonokuhle Ndlovu

should be an issue of individual accommodation versus more radical institutional transformation. This is because persons with disabilities do not need to be accommodated; rather, it should be the social contexts that should be totally transformed so that all people, including those with disabilities, have access, participate, succeed and in turn contribute to knowledge in higher education. A totally transformed higher education system in which all diverse students, not only those with disabilities, are catered for, would be most ideal in the South African context, in Africa and globally.

Acknowledgement

This work is based on the research supported wholly by the National Research Foundation of South Africa (Grant Number: 120773).

References

Abbott, A. (1988). *The systems of professions: An essay on the division of expert labour*. The University of Chicago Press.

Badge, J. (2014). *Teacher assessment on performance Standard 1: Professional knowledge*. Georgia Department of Education.

Bigge, M. L., & Shermis, S. S. (1999). *Learning theories for teachers*. Harper Collins Publishers.

Carter, N., Bryant-Lukosius, D., DiCenso, A., Blythe, J., & Neville, A. J. (2014). The use of triangulation in qualitative research. *Oncol Nursing Forum, 41*(5), 545–547.

Clarke, L., & Winch. C. (2004). Apprenticeship and applied theoretical knowledge. *Educational Philosophy and Theory, 36*(5), 509–522.

Creswell, J. (2008). *Educational research: Planning, conducting and evaluating quantitative and qualitative research*. Prentice Hall.

De Vaus, D. A. (1986). *Surveys in social research*. Unwin Ltd.

Demirkasimoglu, N. (2010). Defining "teacher professionalism" from different perspectives. *Procedia Social and Behavioural Sciences, 9*, 2047–2051.

Department of Higher Education and Training. (2015). *Revised policy on the minimum requirements for teacher education qualification*. Government Gazette.

Devlin, R., & Pothier, D. (2006). *Critical disability theory: Essays in philosophy, politics and law*. UBC Press.

Dickson, B. (2007). Defining and interpreting professional knowledge in an age of performativity: A Scottish case study. *Australian Journal of Teacher Education, 32*(4), 14–28.

Fitchett, A. (2015). Exploring adaptive co-management as a means to improving accessibility for people with reduced mobility at the University of Witwatersrand. In E. Walton & S. Moonsamy (Eds.), *Making education inclusive* (pp. 130–146). Cambridge Scholars Publishing.

Foucault, M. (1982). The subject and power. In H. L. Dreyfus & P. Rabinow (Eds.), *Appended to Michael Foucault: Beyond structuralism and hermeneutics* (pp. 208–226). University of Chicago Press.

Getzel, E. E., & Thoma, C. A. (2008). Experiences of college students with disabilities and the importance of self-determination in higher education setting. *Career Development for Exceptional Individuals, 31*(2), 77–96.

Improving Processes, Practices and Structures 37

Gubrium, J. F., & Holstein, J. A. (2001). From the individual interview to the interview society. In J. F. Gubrium & J. A. Holstein (Eds.), *Handbook of interview research* (pp. 3–32). SAGE Publications.

Haralambos, M., & Holborn, M. (1991). *Sociology: Themes and perspectives.* Collins Education.

Hargreaves, A. (2000). Four ages of professionalism and professional learning. *Teachers and Teaching: History and Practice, 6*(2), 151–182.

Higgs-Kleyn, N., & Kapelianis, D. (1999). The role of professional codes in regulating ethical conduct. *Journal of Business Ethics, 19*(4), 363–374.

Hosking, D. L. (2008). Critical disability theory. *Disability Studies, 2*(4), 7.

Howell, C. (2006). Disabled students and higher education in South Africa. In B. Watermeyer, L. Swartz, T. Lorenzo, M. Schneider, & M. Priestley (Eds.), *Disability and social change: A South African agenda* (pp. 164–178). HSRC.

Leedy, P. D. (1997). *Practical research: Planning and design* (6th ed). Prentice Hall.

Macdonald, K. M. (1995). *The sociology of the professions.* SAGE Publications.

Matshedisho, K. (2007). Access to higher education for disabled students in South Africa: A contradictory conjuncture of benevolence, rights and the social model of disability. *Disability and Society, 22*(7), 685–699.

Matshedisho, K. (2010). Experiences of disabled students in South Africa: Extending the thinking behind disability support. *South African Journal of Higher Education, 24*(5), 730–744.

Mutanga, O. (2017). Students with disabilities' experience in South African education: A synthesis of literature. *South African Journal of Higher Education, 31*(1), 135–155.

Ndhlovu, F. (2014). *Becoming an African diaspora in Australia: Language, culture, identity.* Palgrave Macmillan.

Ndlovu, S. (2017). Obstacles and opportunities in graduating into professions: The case of a University in South Africa. Unpublished Thesis. University of the Witwatersrand, Johannesburg.

Ndlovu-Gatsheni, S. J. (2001). Imperial hypocrisy, settler colonial double standards and denial of human rights to Africans in colonial Zimbabwe. In N. Bhebe & T. Ranger (Eds.), *The historical dimensions of democracy and human rights in Zimbabwe: Volume one: Precolonial and colonial legacies* (pp. 53–83). University of Zimbabwe Publications.

Ndlovu-Gatsheni, S. J. (2012). *The African neo-colonised world.* CODESRIA Books.

Ndlovu-Gatsheni, S. J. (2013). *Empire, global coloniality and subjectivity.* Berghahn Books.

Odendaal-Magwaza, M., & Farman, R. (1997). Unpublished submission by the University of Natal to Education Portfolio Committee at the public hearing on Draft White Paper 3. *A Programme for Higher Education Transformation at the National Assembly.* Parliament, Cape Town.

Quijano, A. (2000). Coloniality of power, ethnocentrism, and Latin America. *Nepantla, 1*(3), 533–580.

Riddel, S., Tinklin, T., & Wilson, A. (2005). *Disabled students in higher education: Perspectives in widening access and changing policies.* Routledge.

Rusznyak, L. (2015). Knowledge selection in initial teacher education programmes and its implication for curricular coherence. *Journal of Education, 60,* 7–29.

Shalem, Y. (2014). What binds professional judgement? The case of teaching. In M. Young & J. Muller (Eds.), *Knowledge, expertise and the professions* (pp. 93–105). Routledge.

Shay, S. (2013). Conceptualizing curriculum differentiation in higher education: A sociology of knowledge point of view. *British Journal of Sociology of Education*, *34*(4), 563–582.

Shulman, L. (1986). Those who understand knowledge growth in teaching. *Educational Researcher*, *15*(2), 4–14.

Simons, M., & Masschelein, J. (2005). Inclusive education for inclusive pupils: A critical analysis of the government of the exceptional. In S. Tremain (Ed.), *Foucault and the government of disability* (pp. 192–207). The University of Michigan Press.

Swart, E., & Greyling, E. (2011). Participation in higher education: Experiences of students with disabilities. *Acta Academia*, *43*(2), 81–110.

Swartz, L., & Schneider, M. (2006). Tough choices: Disability and social security in South Africa. In B. Watermeyer, L. Swartz, T. Lorenzo, M. Schneider, & M. Priestley (Eds.), *Disability and social change: A South African agenda* (pp. 234–243). HSRC.

Taylor, G., & Runté, R. (1995). *Thinking about teaching: An introduction*. Harcourt Brace.

Test, D. W., Fouler, C. H., Wood, W. M., Brewer, D. M., & Eddy, S. (2005). *A conceptual theory*. Continuum.

Titchkosky, T. (2003). *Disability, self and society*. University of Toronto Press.

Tremain, S. (2005). *Foucault and the government of disability*. The University of Michigan Press.

Welch, T. (2002). Teacher education in South Africa before, during and after apartheid: An overview. In J. Adler & Y. Reed (Eds), *Challenges of teacher development: An investigation of take-up in South Africa* (pp. 17–35), Van Schaik.

Winch, C. (2014). Know-how and knowledge in the professional curriculum. In M. Young & J. Muller (Eds.), *Knowledge, expertise and the professions* (pp. 47–60). Routledge.

Young, M., & Muller, J. (2013). On the powers of powerful knowledge. *Review of Education*, *1*(3), 229–250.

Young, M., & Muller, J. (2014). From the sociology of professions to the sociology of professional knowledge. In M. Young & J. Muller (Eds.), *Knowledge, expertise and the professions* (pp. 3–17). Taylor & Francis.

4 Social Justice in Higher Education

A Quest for Equity, Inclusion and Epistemic Access

Tsediso Michael Makoelle

Introduction

Historically, South African higher education institutions have been segregated according to race and colour. The dawn of the new political dispensation has seen these institutions of higher learning merge to form integrated and comprehensive institutions aimed at making education accessible to all students regardless of race, gender, colour or disability. However, since the merger of those institutions, there has been a slow transformation to see some of these institutions—especially those that were for previously advantaged communities—become fully accessible to previously disadvantaged Blacks. While there has been an increase in the admissions of previously disadvantaged students into these institutions, there are voices that maintain that institutions of higher learning have not fully transformed into inclusive centres of learning. There are questions about epistemic access, norms, values, curriculum and institutional cultures that militate against full integration and inclusion. Lately there have been calls to decolonise the curriculum by transitioning the current Eurocentric curriculum to that which recognises the indigenous knowledge systems (Morreira et al., 2020). In 2001 the Department of Education adopted the White Paper 6 which was aimed at building an integrated and inclusive education system. According to White Paper 6, educational institutions are to recognise diversity by making provision for education that responds to the needs of all students regardless of race, including students with special educational needs and those with disabilities (Republic of South Africa [RSA], 2001).

Therefore, the need to align all higher education programmes with inclusive ideals in terms of programme deliveries and assessment strategies emerged. Universities and institutions of higher learning are faced with the mammoth task of ensuring that teaching and learning in those institutions respond to the needs of all students, including those with diverse abilities and needs. The introduction of inclusive education in higher education will go a long way in ensuring:

*   Education for social justice;
*   Emphasis on human rights as espoused by the law of Kazakhstan;
*   Access to economic viability for all;

DOI: 10.4324/9781003228233-4

40   *Tsediso Michael Makoelle*

- A response to global commitments to make the world an equitable and inclusive society and;
- The embracing of diversity.

The trends in higher education for students with diverse abilities and needs have been illustrated in two ways. Firstly, students attend institutions of higher learning and strive to succeed through minimal support or, secondly, students go through unstructured and unplanned accommodation or inclusion procedures which often put them at risk of poor academic progress. As a signatory to the Convention of the Rights of Persons with Disability, South Africa has to ensure that education institutions of higher learning are made accessible also to students with disabilities (Mutanga, 2018). According to Mutanga (2018), there are about 2.9 million South Africans with disabilities. This constitutes 7.5% of the total population of which 1% makes up part of the student population in educational institutions. Mutanga (2018, p. 14) concurs with Lotz-Sisitka (2009), Boughey (2005) and Cross (2018) that, "Proper inclusion implies multidimensional support that is financial, social and academic in nature and extends to policies. It is not enough to consider physical access and the very presence of students with disabilities 'inclusive'".

Therefore, this chapter conceptualises inclusion within the context of higher education, discusses factors inhibiting the promotion of access to institutions of higher learning, synthesises some approaches to developing an inclusive teaching and learning within higher education institutions and draws lessons on how institutions of higher learning can be transformed to be centres of inclusive teaching, pedagogy and learning.

Theoretical Underpinning of Critical Realist Lens

In order to understand inclusion and exclusion within the South African higher education context, one needs to do a deeper analysis of the underlying relational mechanisms that are at play. Critical realism therefore offers an instrumental theoretical compass to unmask and unearth such causal and relational aspects militating against genuine inclusion. The principle of Roy Bhaskar's stratified reality becomes significant in order to unpack the social reality within the higher education sector of South Africa (Bhaskar, 1978). For the purpose of analysis, the domains of reality, that is, empirical, actual and real, are used as magnifying lenses to understand the reality of inclusion and exclusion within the institutions of higher learning in South Africa. The empirical domain represents aspects of human experience through senses, that is, the world as humans see it. The empirical world may not be the actual representation of reality but human lived experiences. The actual domain in constituted by that which occurs around humans but outside their perceptual recognition. The real domain is composed of the underlying relational mechanisms with causal powers which may influence the events at the domains of empirical and actual. These causal mechanisms may or may not be exercised at one particular moment (Bhaskar, 1978).

The real domain is independent of the other two domains. In critical realist contention, the causal relations play a significant role in how the underlying mechanisms are used to influence the actual and empirical reality once executed. The exercise of mechanisms at the domain of real occurs within the framework of agent-agency-social structure equation. The duality of social structure means the agent within the social structure exercises agency to influence the social structure which in turn has a constraining effect on the agent. This duality is critical at it shows how relational and causal mechanisms are always at play in determining reality at any given moment. Therefore, in this chapter I am using the stratified reality dimension to unpack the social reality in institutions of higher learning regarding inclusive and exclusive tendencies. The domain of empirical constitutes the pseudo-inclusive practices experienced by students at these institutions, that is, their admission into programmes, and the superficial tallying of statistics of race, gender or disability as observed and seen. These are done to masquerade as integration and inclusion whereas in actual essence real inclusion has not been achieved. The domain of the actual represents events that occur within the institution of higher learning which are beyond the perceptual recognition of students, that is, the purpose of the curriculum, and the institutional values, norms, customs and traditions embedded into academic practice. The domain of real is composed of the underlying relational mechanisms which, when excursive, may influence the empirical and real domains. These are hidden causal mechanisms such as powers held by those who determine knowledge, who gets access to which knowledges and for a specific purpose. The holders of such causal mechanism may act to influence knowledge and practice, and thus maintain tendencies that are aimed at excluding or pursuing a colonising discourse. Figure 4.1 below provides a schematic representation of the stratified reality in institutions of higher learning according to a critical realist domain of reality (Bhaskar, 1978).

Conceptualising Social Justice and Inclusive Education

The distribution of opportunities to all people such that all have a probable chance of success is referred to as *social justice*. Therefore, social justice education is assumed to be a provision of an equitable and quality education such that all students are provided with equal and equitable educational opportunities to succeed. According to Shaeffer (2019), and echoed by Gerrard (2006), education has a better chance of achieving social justice if it is inclusive and recognises student diversity. This fact is further emphasised by Polat (2011) who avers that inclusion is a first step towards social justice. In this chapter, to illustrate the intersection between inclusion and social justice, Dyson's discourses of inclusion (as cited in Artiles et al., 2006) are used to unpack social justice views within inclusion. Dyson (as cited in Artiles et al., 2006) distinguishes between two main discourses of inclusion (see Figure 4.2).

42 *Tsediso Michael Makoelle*

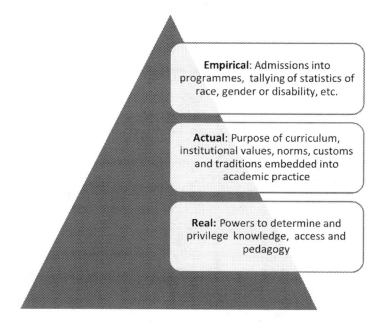

Figure 4.1 Stratified representation of reality in institutions of higher learning.

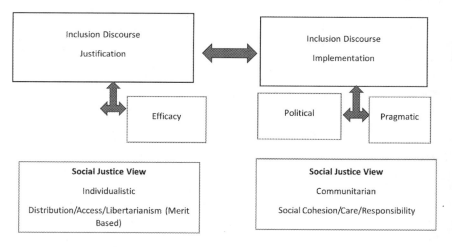

Figure 4.2 Dyson's schematic representation of inclusion discourses and underlying social justice views

Source: Adapted from Artiles et al. (2006).

Firstly, I consider the discourse of justification which advocates for human rights, ethics and efficacy. According to Artiles et al. (2006) this discourse of inclusion tends to lend itself to a social justice view that focuses on access and the redistribution of resources, whilst treating individuals on the basis of merit. This view of social justice has limitations in that it emphasises the

Social Justice in Higher Education 43

individual and fails to recognise the changes that are needed in a specific context. Secondly, the discourse of implementation tends to put more emphasis on the political context and the pragmatic implementation of inclusive measures. This discourse assumes a communitarian view of social justice in that it emphasises a social model that advocates social cohesion, care and collective vision as well as collaborative institutional culture. Inclusion is viewed as the responsibility of the collective. Artiles et al. (2006) argue that in conceptualising social justice within inclusion, a balance between individualistic and communitarian views of social justice is important. Social justice is a foundation on which inclusive education is based.

Although the definition of inclusive education is varied and not universal, the concept emerged out of a need to provide equitable and quality education to all students, regardless of their background (Ainscow, 2010; Makoelle, 2014a). The concept is a critique of special education which was meant to provide education for those assumed to exhibit special needs or disabilities. While the provisions of special education formed and continue to form the significant strand within inclusive education, it is basically a flawed assumption to equate and define inclusive education as education for students with disabilities. Disability is but one narrow stream within the broader inclusive education concept. Ellison (2008) postulates that the special education discourse continues to have a profound influence on modern conceptions of equity and inclusion. Graham and Slee (2008), in an Australian context, cautioned about misconstruing the integration of students with disabilities in the mainstream of education as the success of achieving an inclusive education system. In reality, inclusive education is broader than just repositioning a student with a disability within the education system.

The conceptualisation of inclusive education has been influenced by the theoretical positions people take in understanding the concept. According to Clough and Corbett (2000), there are five key theoretical orientations that have influenced trends in the understanding of inclusive education, namely, psycho-medical, sociological, curriculum, school improvement and disability. However, the psycho-medical and sociological models have been dominant.

Psycho-medical model: This model starts from a deficit assumption about the student. The student is seen through the lens of a medical diagnosis which warrants a special kind of education to address this need. The *sociological model* is a critique of the psycho-medical approach in that special need is regarded as socially constructed. This model laments the negative effect of labelling or grouping students into any sets of categories. The international trend has been tilted towards moving away from the psycho-medical model to the sociological model. However, the South African institutions of higher learning have been pursuing a psycho-medical model. The fact that students are identified with special educational needs and segregated into so-called disability centres shows how far the system of higher education still is from embracing education that is integrated and inclusive. However, the transition from traditional segregating and exclusive practice would require that institutions of higher learning to identify the barriers to full inclusion and address those systematically.

44 Tsediso Michael Makoelle

Challenges of Implementing Inclusive Education in Higher Education

To implement inclusive education in higher education institutions calls for some structural changes, adjustments and modifications to enable students with diverse abilities and needs to benefit and receive quality education.

Dealing with Structural Constraints: The goal of inclusive education is to provide education to all students regardless of their background such as disability, gender, language, race, ethnicity, and socio-economic status in a less restrictive environment.

Architectural Changes: The institution has to make some architectural changes and modifications in the planning of physical space and provide resources that could enhance access, for example, provision of ramps for wheelchairs, and assistive devices in lecture halls (Makoelle, 2014b).

Transforming Institutional Culture: This involves changing institutional values, traditions, social and political relationships and worldview created, shared and transformed by a group of people bound together by a combination of factors that can include a common history, geographical location, language, social class and religion (Nieto, 1999, p. 6).

Enhancing Resilience Through Student Agency: Resilience is known to be the capacity of individuals to negotiate and navigate their pathways towards the resources that sustain well-being, and the capacity of the individuals to share health promoting resources (Ungar, 2005).

Enhancing the Application of Inclusive Pedagogies: *Inclusive pedagogy* is conceptualised as the totality of teaching, learning, beliefs and attitudes facilitating the process of knowing (Florian & Kershner, 2009; Makoelle, 2014c). It is a pedagogy that seeks to be emancipatory, embraces differences, aims to empower, is non-judgmental and starts from the premise that students can learn but differently at their own pace and style. Inclusive pedagogy asks questions about how teaching and learning, assessment, learning environment and the teacher's beliefs, values and attitudes could be altered in order to respond to the diverse abilities and needs of students. Unlike special education pedagogy, which seeks to change the student or address the student's deficit to fit into the normative assumed right educative environment, inclusive pedagogy ensures that the background characteristics of the student are not a barrier to effective teaching and learning.

Addressing Cognitive Justice in Higher Education: The physical presence of the student in the classroom cannot be equated to automatic inclusion. The provision of new knowledge is mediated by the cultural capital of the student, thus equitable learning is central in the epistemological access and inclusion within the pedagogic discourse. Visvanathan coined the concept of cognitive justice in 1997 (Visvanathan, 2016). The concept came about as a result of a concern that Western forms of knowledge and the way knowledge is acquired and validated seemed to perpetuate the dominant hegemonic discourse of the Western cultures (Makoelle, 2014b). Therefore, cognitive justice is a paradigm that seeks to critique the hegemonic paradigm of modern science. It proposes to give recognition to alternative paradigms, especially

Social Justice in Higher Education 45

those that are derived from indigenous forms of knowledge. According to Odora Hoppers (2010, 2012) and Van der Westhuizen (as cited in Odora Hoppers & Richards, 2011), indigenous forms of knowledge have to be part of the knowledge production process and they should not be subjected to standards and should not be forced to fit structures of Western knowledge. This will result in what could be called the *equity of epistemologies*. Kumalo (2020) talks about the significance of using Black archives of knowledge to resurrect the African-ness in the knowledge economy. Similarly, Hlatshwayo et al. (2020) suggest Ubuntu as a critical framework for the decolonisation of the curriculum. They postulate that "Ubuntu currere can be emancipatory alternative to the traditional top-down, hierarchical approach to designing, teaching, and assessing curricula, research and community engagement" (p. 1).

Therefore, this will ensure equitable learning which is a process of bridging the learning gap between those who are advantaged and those disadvantaged in terms of educational resources (United Nations Economic, Scientific and Cultural Organisation [UNESCO], 2012). However, most arguments being put forth for equitable learning focus primarily on access to educational resources; very little is said and done about making *learning itself an emancipatory process*. It is emancipatory in the sense that those indigenous knowledge systems are recognised and incorporated into the teaching and learning process to ensure cognitive justice (Makoelle, 2014c).

Knowledge Economy and Equity: The choice of the methods to produce knowledge, the knowledges prioritised, for example, in curriculum development for programmes, is a tool that could be used to exclude. The choice of what constitutes a curriculum is fundamental and goes a long way in ensuring equity and access. Some form of knowledges can be colonising and disenfranchising. The knowledge holder can monopolise knowledge because they are holding keys or epistemic tools. In his work *The Structuring of Pedagogic Discourse*, Bernstein (2003) talks about autonomous and market-oriented visible pedagogies. Bernstein makes a clear distinction between visible pedagogies that are autonomous which pursue knowledge for its value and dependent visible pedagogies which are dependent on their market relevance (born out of context of cost-effective education). Because these are assumed to be creating jobs, their knowledge tends to be prioritised, leading to reproduction of hierarchies within and among institutions which have great potential for exclusive tendencies (Makoelle, 2014a).

Privatisation and Commodification of Higher Education: The cost of higher education can be a serious barrier to access and inclusion. There are tendencies to privatise higher education and treat it as a commodity for those who can afford it. This leads to mass enrolments geared towards profiteering which may exclude the needy students from low income households and can provide a fertile ground for marginalisation and exclusion (Makoelle, 2014c). However, Walton et al. (2015, p. 263) posit that there is a "need to acknowledge that injections of finance may secure access, but do not necessarily secure success" which means that financial support alone cannot guarantee

46 *Tsediso Michael Makoelle*

success. Based on these challenges and others, the institutions of higher learning have to develop strategies to deal with these issues. The main question would be: How can institutions of higher learning be more inclusive?

Developing an Inclusive Higher Learning Institution

Many institutions of higher learning within Western contexts have established what they term "Disability Centres" or "Disability Units". However, their focus was on students with disabilities and in many cases they have not transformed their role to broaden their scope of function beyond disability to other forms of exclusion. There is a need to move away from this approach to the one that recognises that diversity goes beyond disability. I will therefore in this case advocate for the establishment of "inclusion, equity and access centres" which will focus on the varied nature of diversity.

The development of an inclusive higher learning institution has to begin with the development of clear inclusive education policy guided by achievable goals (Makoelle, 2014b). Firstly, the policy has to start with a clear *vision* which is an ideal state of where the institution wants to be but has not yet achieved. Secondly, the vision is then translated into the *mission* that encompasses the tangible actions the institution should take in its daily operations to ensure the aims encapsulated in the vision are attained. The policy must then be clear on the governance structures for the implementation of inclusive goals. Each school/department in the institution may establish a *school/ departmental-based support team* composed of a school head, member of teaching and learning committee, manager for student services, librarian, faculty member (usually a specialist on inclusive education), teaching assistant and student representatives. These teams will then be part of the establishment of the *institution-based support team* which deals with issues of equity, access and inclusion at an institutional level. The Figure 4.3 is a simplified structure of inclusion, equity and access in an institution of higher learning:

The role of school and institution-based support teams is to, among others:

- Review the policy on inclusion on an annual basis;
- Ensure that marketing and recruitment of students take into account the diverse potential student population from which the institution draws its students;
- Advise institution/university management on possible implications of admission of students with disabilities;
- Establish through interviews or appropriate methods the support needs of students with disabilities or special needs;
- Ensure that there are reasonable plans in place to deal with students who might be academically challenged once accepted into the programme or during the course of the programme;
- Identify students at risk and those that will require additional support;
- Take reasonable steps to ensure that in the selection process all potential students, staff and faculty are not unfairly discriminated against or prejudiced;

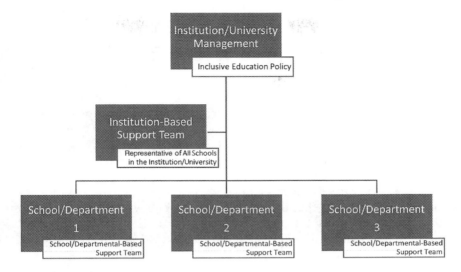

Figure 4.3 Higher education institution inclusive structure.

- Take reasonable actions to ensure both equity and equality during the recruitment process;
- Employ reasonable measures to ensure the infrastructure of the school is accessible to all students, including those with disabilities;
- Through the Teaching and Learning Committee, take reasonable measures to ensure access to teaching and material by all students, including those with disabilities;
- Make all assistive devices available to students so that they are not disadvantaged;
- Ensure assessment practices are appropriate to the diverse abilities and needs of students and that alternative forms of assessment could be explored in keeping with the principle of support;
- Make sure that pedagogy in the lectures is inclusive by encouraging and empowering faculty on principles, practices, approaches and strategies for accommodating diverse students' needs.

The above functions and roles have to take into cognisance the context and the situation at every institution of higher learning. It is important that the collaboration of all stakeholders become central to all activities aimed at including all students and making sure that all students have access, thus enabling participation in equitable teaching and learning that responds to the needs of all students.

Developing a Teaching and Learning Strategy

To develop an inclusive strategy at an institution of higher learning will require a systematic transformation and reforming of the process of teaching and learning. Several authors provide different approaches as to how an inclusive teaching and learning environment could be achieved. Cross (2018) discusses the constraining effect of institutional culture, that is, practices, norms and values, as instrumental in restricting epistemological access. He makes a distinction between "formal access" which merely represents student admissions in the university programme and "epistemological access" as the ability of students to make meaningful success out of participation in the academic practice. According to Boughey (2005), epistemological access can be achieved only when the university understands the cultural capital new students bring in the process of teaching and learning. Therefore, epistemological access is viewed as critical for enhancing and broadening student participation. This view is echoed by Lotz-Sisitka (2009, p. 1) quoting Morrow (2007), by postulating that the aim of teaching and learning should be to enable epistemological access to knowledge in the modern world. Lotz-Sisitka argues that enemies of epistemological access remain the empiricist epistemologies and relativist epistemologies. She proposes that a realist epistemology is required if epistemological access is to be realised within the South African higher education context.

Various authors have suggested how epistemic access could be achieved. For instance, Walton (2018) postulates that inclusive education could be a vehicle for decolonising education in South Africa as it resonates with the Afrocentric principle and philosophy of life, that is, Ubuntu. She argues that any decolonising project in higher education should dispel Eurocentric approaches and embody the African approach. Going further in this process is viewed by Rowe et al. (2010) as a process that must take into account the students' voices. In their investigation of the role of students giving feedback about inclusive practices within their academic engagements, they argue for a need to hear student feedback from the perspectives of inclusion and support which more often than not is a neglected area. The role of students is emphasised by Cerasnova (2018) who avers that a student-centred approach is fundamental for building an inclusive pedagogical environment.

Hockings (2010) synthesised literature on inclusive teaching and learning in higher education. In this synthesis Hockings draws some conclusions; among them is that pedagogy, curricula and assessment are the cornerstones of making student learning meaningful, relevant and accessible. This means that teaching and learning must assume a pedagogy that is inclusive, deliver a curriculum that takes into account student diversity and ensure that assessment responds to the diverse needs of students.

Conclusion and Recommendations

Using Bhaskar's (1978) stratified reality analogy, several conclusions are drawn regarding equity and inclusion within the institutions of higher learning in South Africa. The indication is that inclusion is implemented superficially. Firstly, at the level of empirical reality, the analysis shows that although there has been an increase in student enrolments from previously disadvantaged groups, this has not translated into increased epistemic access. According to Cross (2018), students from these groups are likely to make slow academic progress or drop out completely from programmes. Furthermore, the institutions of higher learning seem to have not made the transition from understanding inclusion as an integrated approach to teaching and learning rather than segregation of students to disability centres. Therefore, a paradigm shift from the medical to the social model of inclusion seems imminent and necessary.

Secondly, at the level of actual reality, it is evident that educational infrastructure of these institutions was not developed with inclusion of diverse students in mind; as a result, more structural adjustments are needed to accommodate diversity. While the curriculum is delivered to all students, there are voices that call for the curriculum to be decolonised. The current curriculum does not take into account the indigenous knowledge systems and is also heavily Eurocentric. There are calls to decolonise the curriculum and Africanise institutions of higher learning in order to enhance student cognitive justice. While there are attempts to transition to an inclusive pedagogy that recognises diversity, it seems as though there is inflexibility and rigidity towards reform and change, for instance, assessment practices are still heavily standardised with a total disregard for the students' uniqueness and differences in learning.

Thirdly, in reality it seems as though there are underlying relational mechanisms which are at play, that is, superficial inclusion is meant as a tool to exclude the marginalised from actual inclusion which can make them access genuine education that might actually lead to their empowerment. There are underlying intentions to maintain intellectual dominance and power by those who enjoyed the privileges of access to empowering education. The non-transformation of culture, norms, values, traditions and customs at institutions of higher learning serve as a barrier to real empowerment for the disenfranchised and therefore constitutes the reality in the South African higher education context.

References

Ainscow, M. (2010). Achieving excellence and equity: Reflections on the development of practices in one local district over 10 years, *An International Journal of Research, Policy and Practice, 21*(1), 75–92.

Artiles, A. J., Harris-Murri, N., & Rostenberg, D. (2006). Inclusion as social justice: Critical notes on discourses, assumptions, and the road ahead. *Theory into Practice, 45*(3), 260–268.

Bernstein, B. (2003). *Class, codes and control (Vol. 4): The structuring of pedagogic discourse*. Routledge.

Bhaskar, R. (1978). *A realist theory of science* (2nd ed.). Harvester Press.

Boughey, C. (2005). Epistemological access to the university: An alternative perspective. *South African Journal of Higher Education, 19*(3), 230–242. https://doi.org/10.4314/sajhe.v19i3.25516

Cerasnova, Z. (2018). *Inclusive higher education*. Nakladatelství Gasset.

50   *Tsediso Michael Makoelle*

Clough, P., & Corbett, J. (2000). *Theories of inclusive education: a student's guide.* SAGE Publications.

Cross, M. (2018). *Steering epistemic access in higher education in South Africa: Institutional dilemmas.* Ciudad Autónoma de Buenos Aires: CLACSO.

Ellison, C. (2008). *Children and adolescents with special needs.* Centre for Excellence for Children and Adolescents with Special Needs: University of Northern British Columbia.

Florian, L., & Kershner, R. (2009). Inclusive pedagogy. In H. Daniels, H. Lauder & J. Porter (Eds.), *Knowledge, values and educational policy: A critical perspective* (pp. 173–183). Routledge.

Gerrard, L. C. (2006). Inclusive education: An issue of social justice, *Equity and Excellence in Education, 27*(1), 58–67.

Graham, L. J., & Slee, R. (2008). An illusory interiority: Interrogating the discourse/s of inclusion. *Educational Philosophy and Theory, 40*(2), 277–293. https://doi.org/10.1111/j.1469-5812.2007.00331.x

Hlatshwayo, M. N., Shawa, L. B., & Nxumalo, S. A. (2020). Ubuntu *currere* in the academy: A case study from the South African experience, *Third World Thematics: A TWQ Journal, 5*(1–2), 120–136. https://doi.org/10.1080/23802014.2020.1762509

Hockings, C. (2010). *Inclusive learning and teaching in higher education: A synthesis of research.* https://www.advance-he.ac.uk/knowledge-hub/inclusive-learning-and-teaching-higher-education-synthesis-research

Kumalo, S. H. (2020). Resurrecting the black archive through the decolonisation of philosophy in South Africa. *Third World Thematics: A TWQ Journal, 5*(1–2), 19–36, https://doi.org/10.1080/23802014.2020.1798276

Lotz-Sisitka, H. (2009). Epistemological access as an open question in education. *Journal of Education, 46*, 57–79.

Makoelle, T. M. (2014a). Pedagogy of inclusion: A quest for social justice and sustainable learning environments. *Mediterranean Journal of Social Sciences, 5*(17), 1257–1269.

Makoelle, T. M. (2014b). Cognitive justice: A road map for equitable inclusive learning environments. *International Journal of Education and Research, 2*(7), 505–518.

Makoelle, T. M. (2014c, 21 August). Inclusion in higher education: A quest for epistemic access. Presented at SOTL Seminar, University of Johannesburg.

Morreira, S., Luckett, K., Kumalo, S. H., & Ramgotra, M. (2020). Confronting the complexities of decolonising curricula and pedagogy in higher education. *Third World Thematics: A TWQ Journal, 5*(1–2), 1–18. https://doi.org/10.1080/23802014.2020.1798278

Mutanga, O. (2018). *South Africa's universities can do more to make disabled students feel included.* https://theconversation.com/south-africas-universities-can-do-more-to-make-disabled-students-feel-included-70672

Nieto, S. (1999). Placing equity front and centre: Some thoughts on transforming teacher education for a new century. *Journal of Teacher Education, 51*(3), 180–187.

Odora Hoppers, C. A. (2010). Emerging African perspectives on values in a globalizing world. In K. Sporre & J. Mannberg (Eds.), *Values, religions and education in changing societies* (pp. 147–156). Springer.

Odora Hoppers, C. A. (2012). *Indigenous knowledge and the integration of knowledge systems: Towards a philosophy of articulation* (2nd ed.). New Africa Books.

Odora Hoppers, C. A., & Richards, H. (2011). *Rethinking thinking: modernity's "other" and the transformation of the university.* Taproot Series (Vol. 1). University of South Africa.

Polat, F. (2011). Inclusion in education: A step towards social justice. *International Journal of Educational Development, 31*(1), 50–58.

Republic of South Africa (RSA). (2001). *Education White Paper 6 Special Needs Education: Building an inclusive education and training system.* Government Printers.

Rowe, A. D., Muchatuta, M., & Wood, L. N. (2010). *Inclusive practice in higher education: Feedback that breaks pedagogical barriers.* http://www.researchgate.net

Shaeffer, S. (2019). Inclusive education: a prerequisite for equity and social justice, *Asia Pacific Education Review, 20,* 181–192.

Ungar, M. (2005). Pathways to resilience among children in child welfare, corrections, mental health and educational settings: Navigation and negotiation. *Child & Youth Care Forum, 34*(6), 423–444.

United Nations Educational, Scientific and Cultural Organisation (UNESCO). (2012). *Education for all global monitoring report.* UNESCO.

Visvanathan, S. (2016). *The search for cognitive justice.* http://www.india-seminar.com/2009/597/597_shiv_visvanathan.htm

Walton, E. (2018). Decolonising (through) inclusive education? *Educational Research for Social Change, 7*(Special Issue), 31–45.

Walton, E., Bosman, B., & Osman, R. (2015). Promoting access to higher education in an unequal society. *South African Journal of Higher Education, 29*(1), 262–269.

5 Decolonising African University Teaching by Unyoking Deaf Culture from Disability

Martin Musengi

Introduction

Universities have tended to filter their understanding of the condition of being deaf through a pathological model that views deafness as a disability in need of remediation. Most university systems believe that deaf people are, at least in a physiological sense, inferior to hearing people as they patronise those who are deaf who aspire to university education. Universities usually assess the extent to which their curricula can remediate deaf students so that they can teach them the same things in the same way as hearing students. This approach of viewing deafness as a communication disability in a largely hearing world is colonial as it attempts to assimilate them to a dominant hearing culture. It is the antithesis of the United Nations Sustainable Development Goal (UN SDG) 4 with its thrust of celebrating diversity and providing quality, inclusive education for all, including those who are deaf. This chapter argues that the African context of protest and struggle against colonialism should place African universities at the forefront of open-minded recognition and celebration of diversity. The chapter analyses the paradox of African university curricula that remain in colonial mode with regard to students who ought to be considered as culturally Deaf rather than deaf and disabled. At this point, it may be prudent to note how capital letter "D" and small letter "d" in the word "deaf" are consistently used in this chapter. The chapter follows a convention started by Woodward (1972) which uses capital letter "D" in "Deaf" to denote a cultural condition and lower case "d" in "deaf" to denote the physical condition of not hearing, that is, a disability. In this convention, the capitalised form "Deaf" is used to refer to people who share a sign language and cultural values that are distinct from hearing society. Lowercase "deaf" is used to refer to the audiological condition of deafness which is considered pathological rather than cultural. On the basis of this convention, the chapter discusses the philosophy and practices that colonise education for students who are usually assumed to be deaf when they could be Deaf. It examines principles, strategies and practices that can be used to reverse this trend and decolonise university education through an African view of the person. The chapter proposes curricula considerations that could propel African university education to the forefront of showcasing inclusive

DOI: 10.4324/9781003228233-5

Unyoking Deaf Culture from Disability 53

education as a construct for liberation rather than domestication, for celebrating diversity rather than assimilation, and for decolonising rather than colonising others.

Models of Disability and the Colonial Meaning of Teaching in University

Disability literally means one is "not able" (Andrews et al., 2004). Andrews et al. (2004) said that the term disability logically leads to a response-set in which people view disability as a state of being that is not normal, reflecting loss, weaknesses, helplessness or heroism in the face of adversity. They argued that this frame of reference is bound to encourage ambivalence towards disability, involving both compassion and not caring. In many cultures across the world, the value and meaning of disability in the traditional or moral model is associated with sin, guilt, shame and punishment.

Traditionally, many of the world religions have had doctrines conveying messages about disability. Mallory (1992) cited the example of Palau where all disabilities are believed to be caused by some failure on the part of someone to follow tradition, fulfil a responsibility or appease an ancestor. According to Kaplan (2013), in this model, disability is regarded as a punishment inflicted upon an individual or family by an external force because of misdemeanours committed by the person with a disability, someone in the family or ancestors. Kabzems and Chimedza (2002) analysed the situation in Southern Africa and found that disability continues to be associated with maternal wrongdoing, "sacrificing" a child in exchange for good crops, witchcraft, evil spirits, punishment or a test from God. The latter correlates with ancient Hebrew tradition which taught that each human is an entity created when God's breath entered clay, and that bodily impediments come from God (O'Neill, 2009). Peters and Chimedza (2000) wrote that rituals and spiritual ceremonies are held to cleanse the disabled person and dispel evil spirits from the family. This concurs with Jesus' miracle in Mark 7 verse 32 in which deaf people heard and dumb people spoke (O'Neill, 2009).

Tradition shows differences in the way in which the body and physical characteristics are given value and meaning in different cultures. Charlton (1998) illustrated this by explaining that a facial scar is considered a deformity in much of Western culture but is considered a badge of honour by the Dahomey of Africa. This concurs with the assertion by Devlieger (1998) that Western bio-medical definitions of impairment are not universal and Stone (2001) who said that perceptions of the body and mind vary across cultures and also change over time. Overall, this suggests that the value given to physical characteristics influence traditional attitudes towards disability.

In Western society, what counts as normal or abnormal is medically institutionalised. Foucault (1979) stated that the norm establishes the figure of the normal as a principle of coercion for the figure of the abnormal. This means that medical science has the power to determine what is normal and to force whatever it perceives as abnormal to try to live up to the standards of

54   *Martin Musengi*

the normal. These Foucauldian ideas about such a norm usually abstract this or that feature of the lone individual and make it the defining or essential characteristic which entities aspiring to the description "person" must have. The individualistic medical approach to disability is rooted in the work of sociologist Talcott Parsons and his discussion of sickness and sickness-related behaviour (Barnes, 1998; Barnes & Mercer, 2005). Parsons is reported to have argued that the "normal" state of being in Western society is good health, and therefore sickness, and by implication any impairments, are deviations from "normality". Foucault said that medicine dictates what constitutes normal, thereby identifying a whole class of deviant individuals.

This institutionalisation of the norm, which Foucault called normalisation, indicates the pervasive standards that structure and define social meaning (Feder, 2013). The medical model embodies what Parsons called the *sick role* which is a view of clients as patients exempt from normal social roles as they are not responsible for their condition. In this view, people with disabilities are defined as pathological and in need of cure. The *International Classification of Disease* ICD-10-CM (World Health Organisation [WHO], 2014) and the *Diagnostic and Statistical Manual* (American Psychological Association [APA], 2013) provide common terminology for medicine and psychiatry respectively, and so a comparable taxonomy of disability was deemed necessary to systematise documentation. The *International Classification of Impairments, Disabilities and Handicaps* (ICDH) (WHO, 1980, 2002) are documents published to accompany the ICD-10-CM to document the consequences of disease and injury. Central to the ICDH classification is the understanding that impairment denotes any loss or abnormality of psychological, physiological or anatomical structure or function, while disability is any restriction or lack (resulting from impairment) of ability to perform an activity in the manner or within the range considered normal for a human being. In this thinking, handicap is a disadvantage for any person, resulting from impairment or disability that limits or prevents the fulfilment of a role that is normal for that person depending on age, sex, social and cultural factors. This means that disease can lead to impairment which can lead to disability which in turn can lead to handicap.

When a "hearing" norm has been defined as essential, this results in what Lane (1999) called an infirmity model of deafness but which most of the scientific literature calls a pathological or disability model of deafness (Munoz-Baell & Ruiz, 2000; Rose, 1995; Torres, 1995). Munoz-Baell and Ruiz (2000) wrote that professional intervention from this point of view is concerned with the communicative disability and its implications for the deaf person.

The normalising power of medical science, however, can be resisted, for example, by resisting an audiological understanding of deafness as hearing impairment. Resisting this normalising power from audiology is based on a social model of disability and results in what Foucault (1990) called a reverse discourse. As an illustration of reverse discourse, Foucault (1990) gave the example of how the normalising power which made the homosexual person an object of psychiatric medicine also produced the improbable concept of "gay

Unyoking Deaf Culture from Disability   55

pride". In the same way, the normalising power of medicine and Western culture can be resisted and normality recast. Baumann and Murray (2009) referred to reframing or recasting of deaf into Deaf gain, which is a form of sensory and cognitive diversity having the potential to contribute to the greater good of humanity (Baumann & Murray, 2009). Using the social model of disability, Baumann and Murray (2009) showed how Deaf gain is a view which recasts Deaf people as normal. In this model, deaf people are presented as colonised subjects (Ladd, 2003), targets of audism, which is akin to racism as it evaluates deaf people's intelligence and behaviour according to how well they can approximate the speech and behaviours of hearing people (Humphries, 1977).

Colonialism is cultural, educational and political change in line with the coloniser's needs and the social structures that strengthen the coloniser's power (Bauman, 2004). Education is a power site of hegemonic control where the colonised, subaltern community is assimilated into the coloniser's way of thinking and seeing the world (Spivak, 1999). Wa Thiong'o (1986) argued that this colonialism of the mind and imagination is the worst form of domination hidden in institutions and discourses that govern the globe. Most significant in this regard is the dual character of language, both as a means of communication and a carrier of culture. In this case, sign language is stripped of its history and culture in order to entrench a spoken language as part of the legitimation of audism in the colonial discourse in education of the deaf (Weber, 2015). Not only is language essential to who we are, our place and being or ontology, it also encodes the epistemology of our world. Ndlovu-Gatsheni (2013) made the epistemic link that schools, colleges, universities and churches in Africa are sites for the reproduction of coloniality. In this light, the meaning of teaching for university teachers is influenced by the model of being deaf that the university teachers internalise within the university as a community of practice.

Teachers in universities are what Lave and Wenger (1991) called a community of practice in that as a group they create norms and values and have a shared understanding that binds them together. These are processes that Wenger (1998) said are critical in determining a community of practice. University lecturers are socialised formally and informally into the practice of teaching. In Wenger's (1998) terms, they negotiate the meaning of what they do through continuously interacting with others in processes of give-and-take on a day-to-day basis. Give-and-take implies that university lecturers negotiate the meaning of their teaching experience with deaf students, other teachers in the university and outsiders in a world of both resistance and malleability.

University teachers informed by traditional attitudes could believe that deafness is caused by failure on the part of someone to fulfil certain responsibilities and so might devalue it and give it meaning in light of traditional response sets to disability. Although Kaplan (2013) stated that the traditional moral model is less prevalent nowadays, it is possible that some teachers in universities are socialised to view disability as a punishment inflicted by an external force. Their responsibility to disabled people may therefore arise from a mystical commitment which sees no difference between what they are

56   *Martin Musengi*

supposed to do and what religious leaders do as they cleanse and heal. Teaching based on the traditional moral model could be seen as a vocation commissioned and guided by direct divine intervention (Flanagan, 2003). Such a perception is congruent with attempting to make deaf people hear and dumb persons speak, or at least offer them an education out of pity, since they are seen as deficient or medically pathological.

The Medical Pathological Understanding of Deafness

When university lecturers are malleable to infirmity model-based norms, they filter their understanding of deafness through the medical discourse of disability and espouse knowledge and beliefs about teaching deaf students consistent with this discourse. They might, for example, think of deafness mainly in terms of hearing loss and deficiency. Teaching that is filtered through a pathological model is undergirded by the belief that deafness is a condition characterised by an auditory deficit. Reagan (1995) stated that many believe that deaf people are, at least in a physiological sense, inferior to hearing people. University teachers in this frame of mind are likely to pity and patronise their deaf students whom they view as having a hearing loss or impairment. They may then naturally try to remediate the deficits, for example, through encouraging the use of hearing aids (Reagan, 1995). Such teaching is done so that the hearing impairment does not result in a communication disability and handicap in a largely hearing and speaking world.

In addition, university educators might believe deaf people to be socially isolated, intellectually weak, behaviourally impulsive and emotionally immature (Lane, 1999). University teachers could then believe that such impulsive behaviour was attributable to inadequate social training or mental illness as deaf people are supposed to share the same cultural knowledge, experiences and meanings as hearing people. This is a phenomenon which Siple (1994) called an assumption of similarity; hearing service providers steeped in the pathological model believe that the only difference between Deaf and non-deaf people is that Deaf people cannot hear. They assume that deaf people's behavioural deviance coupled with the communication disability would result in a disadvantage or handicap in learning. Such a handicap is viewed as especially possible in a society dominated by hearing and speaking. This personal tragedy approach (Oliver, 2009) is characterised by perceptions of the dependence of disabled people and stereotypes which evoke pity, fear and patronising attitudes. This approach is contrasted with the social model of disability.

The Social Understanding of Disability and Deafness

The social model is based on the idea that disability is not a result of impairment but a direct consequence of society's failure to take into account the differing needs of people with disabilities and remove barriers they encounter (Oliver, 2009). Disability is something imposed on people's impairments through stereotyping, prejudice, discrimination and lack of access. According to Berghs et al. (2020), the social model developed from the experiences of people with disabilities and their activism against the traditional charity and medical models of disability. People with disabilities resisted the control that non-disabled professionals using charity and medical approaches had over their lives. They fought to remove the focus and "blame" from themselves as individuals with disabilities to society generally. Globally, the resistance blossomed into a disability rights movement, Disabled People's International (DPI) with its mantra "Nothing about us, without us" (Charlton, 1998).

The establishment of DPI in Winnipeg in 1980, involving representatives of organisations of disabled people from both the developing and developed world, marked a major milestone in the development of the global disability movement and of regional movements. According to Manombe-Ncube (2016), at no other time did professionals and philanthropists face such a major challenge to their dominance in the disability field by the disabled people themselves. This indeed marked a paradigm shift from service provision by philanthropists, to the articulation of disability as a human rights and development issue, and the demand for equal participation and inclusion of disabled people in all issues concerning them. The United Nations' declaration of 1981 as the International Year of Disabled Persons and 1983 to 1992 as the UN Decade on the World Programme of Action Concerning Disabled Persons, served to bring visibility to the social model views of disability issues.

The UN Decade on the World Programme of Action Concerning Disabled Persons also coincided with the final stages of popular struggles against authoritarian and colonialist regimes in countries such as Zimbabwe, Namibia, South Africa and Uganda. These popular demands for political and economic change (Camay & Gordon, 1998) also influenced the emergence of the disability movement in Africa, alongside the wider general demand for democracy and the inclusion of marginalised people in the building of new democracies (Manombe-Ncube, 2016). Much as the nationalist liberation struggles in Africa fought to overthrow colonial, imperialist capitalism and replace it with social democracy, disability rights movements also sought to overthrow paternalism and the injustices of neoliberalism brought about by globalisation.

Neoliberal encroachments onto moral and legal entitlements of people with disabilities in Africa infringe many rights. According to Mladenov (2015), neoliberalism insists on expanding the market logic and principles to social policy. As Mladenov (2015) observed, curtailment of social rights focuses on minimisation of universal benefits and services by retrenching the welfare dimension of the state, which is seen as an impediment to the optimal functioning of the markets. Neoliberalism generally increases stigmatisation of disability benefits (Grover & Soldatic, 2013; Soldatic, 2018) in an environment where support for people with disabilities is largely insufficient (Sakellariou & Rotarou, 2017) as "austerity" has become a guide word in policy-making in many countries (Iriarte et al., 2016). The social model of disability is therefore under attack from neoliberalism, but its further development into a socio-cultural understanding of deafness may help it weather the storm.

58 Martin Musengi

Socio-Cultural Model of Deafness in an African View of Personhood

The socio-cultural model is based on the idea that being deaf is not a disability, but that deaf people are a linguistic minority using sign language. This minority is no more in need of individual cures than linguistic minorities anywhere in the world. Reagan (1995) explained that, in this view, deafness is not understood as a disability involving an inability to function audiologically like people with typical hearing, but it is understood with respect to linguistic, social and cultural issues. The socio-cultural understanding of deaf people is consistent with the African, Ubuntu view of "person" espoused by Menkiti (2007).

The Ubuntu view denies that persons can be defined by focusing on this or that particular physical or psychological characteristic of the lone individual (Menkiti, 2007). Rather than focusing on hearing or lack of it, a person is defined by reference to the environing community. As Mbiti (1969, p. 17) noted, the African view of the person can be summed up in the statement: "I am because we are, and since we are, therefore I am." On the basis of this dictum, Menkiti (2007) concluded that, as far as Africans are concerned, the reality of the communal world takes precedence over the reality of individual life histories. From an Ubuntu view therefore, one cannot diminish any other person, disabled or not, without at the same time diminishing oneself. This is evident in African proverbs which are containers of meaning on disability.

The African proverb, *Seka hurema wafa* (Literally meaning laugh at disability after you are dead), implies that one should never laugh at disability as one can get disabled even in old age. Devlieger (1999) stated that this proverb reflects the existential insecurity of laughing at someone with a disability as anyone could become disabled one day. Another proverb, *Chirema ndochine zano, chinotamba chakasendama kumadziro* (A deformed person is clever, he supports himself against a wall when dancing) demonstrates that people with physical disabilities are clever at finding solutions for activities that would seem difficult or impossible. Devlieger (1999) stated that this proverb shows that people with disabilities can have positive experiences, that they also have a drive for survival. These and other proverbs are widely used in the socialisation of African community members and may therefore reflect some of the social input about disability in these communities.

These proverbs are used within the wider context of Ubuntu, the African philosophy of life, whose fundamental belief is *umuntu ngumuntu ngabantu* (a person can only be a person through others) (Mbigi & Maree, 1995). As this philosophy of life advocates embracing others through whom one sees oneself, it fosters acceptance of people with disabilities as well. Edwards et al. (2004) explained that Ubuntu in essence means being honest, accommodative, sharing, saving life at all costs and respecting young and old. These key aspects of Ubuntu resonate with the ideology of the United Nations Educational, Scientific and Cultural Organisation (UNESCO) (1994) on inclusive education, whose basic tenet is a respect for diversity, as well as with the United Nations Convention on the Rights of People with Disabilities (UNCRPD, 2006) and the UN SDG 4.

Unyoking Deaf Culture from Disability 59

In light of traditional positive socialisation on disability in African communities, the contemporary generalised stigmatisation of people with disability in which they are called *chirema*, meaning a burden with thing-like rather than human attributes, is possibly a colonial project. As Ndlovu-Gatsheni (2018) observed, the social and political history of Africa is fundamentally a tale of attempted genocides, epistemicides, linguicides, inventions and standardisations of indigenous languages to accord with Eurocentric linguistic standards for instrumental purposes. The observation by Devlieger (1998) buttressed this with respect to disability-related language. Devlieger (1998) averred that the practice of grouping people together in a recognisable category as "disabled" can be traced back only to the histories and cultural contexts of specific Western societies.

The establishment of colonial languages brought with it much of the disability-related terminology translated into local languages, with the term for physical disability usually becoming generic by acquiring broader meanings which incorporate people with a variety of impairments (Devlieger, 1998). It is uncertain whether deaf people were considered as disabled and therefore a burden in traditional, pre-colonial African society as the experiences of being deaf in that society would not have necessitated the lumping together of the deaf and the physically disabled. Deaf people could contribute economically to traditional communities and so could hardly be considered as a burden and therefore disabled. According to Nhundu (1995), in pre-colonial Africa, personal development was community-driven; it found meaning only when the individual was able to contribute to the development of the community. Kabzems and Chimedza (2002) interpreted this as meaning that individuals were pragmatically accepted according to what they could contribute to the life and welfare of the community. Unfortunately, as Ndlovu-Gatsheni (2018) observed, there are methodological challenges in trying to excavate how colonial encounters interfered with indigenous languages and the pre-colonial harmony that existed.

What is however certain is that, in Africa, it is in rootedness in an ongoing human community that one comes to see oneself as a person, and it is by first knowing this community as a stubborn abiding fact of the psychophysical world that the one comes to know oneself as a durable, more or less permanent, fact of this world (Menkiti, 2007). Menkiti (2007) argued that in the African dictum "I am because we are", the "we" referred to here is not an additive "we" but a thoroughly fused collective "we". It is a collectivity in the truest sense in which there is assumed to be an organic dimension to the relationship between the component individuals. This contrasts with the Western understanding of community, where there is a non-organic bringing together of atomic individuals into a unit more akin to an association than to a community. The primacy of community in Africa is meant to apply not only ontologically, but also in regard to epistemic accessibility.

Epistemic Accessibility for Deaf Students

The primacy of the communal world from the African viewpoint is congruent with the socio-cultural view of deaf people as a linguistic minority bound

60   *Martin Musengi*

together by sign language within Deaf culture. Reagan (1995) explained that sign language acts as a linguistic mediator because its structures and vocabulary provide the framework within which experience is organised, perceived and understood. This means that concepts as understood by Deaf-signing and hearing-speaking people are based on different norms. Biologically, deafness alone can enhance certain aspects of an individual's visual attention (Bavelier et al., 2006). Specifically, deafness causes an individual to allocate more attention to the visual periphery and be more sensitive to motion on the periphery (Hauser et al., 2010). This effect might be due to deaf individuals' intrinsic need, for survival's sake, to rely on the visual modality more than hearing individuals do. There are other influences that are not effects of deafness but effects of competency in a visual language that enhance some cognitive functions (Bellugi et al., 1990; Emmorey & Kosslyn, 1996). On this basis, Hauser et al. (2010) argued that being deaf begets unique additional experiences for deaf individuals that go beyond auditory sensory input. By virtue of their biology, deaf individuals live their lives in a visual reality, which leads to the acquisition of a knowledge base that is different from that of hearing individuals.

In the socio-cultural model, epistemic accessibility is critical in that it is different for Deaf-signing people who have what has been termed Deaf epistemology (Hauser et al., 2010). Hauser et al. (2010) explained that Deaf epistemology constitutes the nature and extent of the knowledge that deaf individuals acquire growing up in a society that relies primarily on audition to navigate life. Deaf culture and Deaf epistemologies are transmitted by Deaf children and Deaf adults who have Deaf parents and who have grown up in a linguistically rich signing environment as well as the far more numerous deaf children of hearing parents in interaction with their various environments (Miller, 2010). Deafness creates beings who are more visually oriented compared to their auditorily oriented peers. The manner in which hearing individuals interact with deaf individuals shapes how deaf individuals acquire knowledge and how they learn. Aspects of the Deaf episteme, not caused by deafness but by Deafhood, have a positive impact on how deaf individuals learn, resist audism, stay healthy, and navigate the world. Citing an example of the Deaf episteme, Padden and Humphries (1988) gave the example that in American Sign Language (ASL) if one signs that a person is VERY HARD-OF-HEARING,[1] it means the person has substantial residual hearing, while A-LITTLE-HARD-OF-HEARING would suggest far less residual hearing. This is the opposite of what the words mean in English and Reagan (1995) explained that this means that the concepts themselves are based on different norms, hence the argument that sign language is mediating experience in a different way.

Pedagogical Implications: The Meaning of Teaching Deaf Students in Universities

The meaning of teaching for teachers subscribing to the traditional/moral model, pathological/medical model or the socio-cultural model of deafness is

Unyoking Deaf Culture from Disability 61

likely to be different. Teaching deaf learners would mean different things to those in these three main models because the teachers' dispositions towards deafness are different. On the one hand, the teacher informed by the traditional model and the pathological model might see eccentric behaviour, inadequate social training or mental illness which needed to be remedied. On the other hand, the teacher informed by the socio-cultural model might see a unique set of knowledge, experience, values and meanings which need to be respected and nurtured. The process of arriving at different meanings of experience is explicated by Wenger (1998).

According to Wenger (1998), teaching is a process by which teachers experience the world and their engagement with it is meaningful. He stated that this kind of meaning does not exist in people or in the world, but in people's dynamic relation in the world. As Wenger (1998, p. 12) noted, "Meaning is not pre-existing, but neither is it simply made up. Negotiated meaning is at once historical, dynamic, contextual and unique." University teachers do not find the meaning of teaching ready-made nor do they simply make it up. They negotiate the meaning of teaching by being amenable to some norms and resisting certain values of some colleagues and community members so that each teacher comes up with experiences and meanings that are unique. Meaning is therefore in experience where it is located in negotiation. Negotiation of meaning involves participation and reification (Wenger, 1998).

Participation means that, as members of the community of practice of university, lecturers have mutual relationships with others and so shape each other's experiences of the meaning of teaching. Reification means that university teachers project their meanings onto teaching and then perceive them as having a reality of their own. For example, abstractions such as "intelligence" or "quality" might be talked about by the lecturers as if they were things, active agents. They might talk about quality in higher education going up or down.

Similarly, university teachers could have fixed quantity or incremental views of intelligence which influence how they view deaf learners' academic potential. As they participate in their communities and reify certain concepts, the lecturers negotiate the meaning of the experience of teaching as well as their identity as educational professionals. They could view what they do on a daily basis from a traditional, medical or socio-cultural understanding. According to Wenger et al. (2002), the individual person is an active participant in the practices of social communities and the construction of their own identity through these communities. To put it another way, university teachers in a community of practice actively participate in the construction of a professional identity which can be pathologically or socio-culturally focussed.

Traditional and pathological models of deafness usually result in educational practices that assume that those who are deaf either have a culturally-hearing identity or aspire to one. These practices are prevalent in universities where sophisticated assistive technology and cochlear implants are thought to be sufficient to enable access to the usual oral lectures. Although there are no clear-cut laws and policies on this in many African universities, their Disability Resource Units usually subscribe to supporting these practices by

62   *Martin Musengi*

stating that they must ensure deaf students have equal access by providing them with assistive hearing devices and by making other procedural changes to accommodate their learning needs. Learning needs that are accommodated usually pertain to enabling speech-reading or improved reception of spoken lectures by providing favourable seating positions. The focus is on trying to enable reception of the spoken language used in lectures either aurally or visually. The possibility that the spoken language may be totally inaccessible is either not considered or, when it is, it is used to conclude that the deaf student cannot undertake studies at that level and therefore justifies their failure or exclusion from studies. The lack of clear-cut policies in addition to lack of resources such as hearing aids often results in deaf students receiving limited or no service to accommodate them in university departments that subscribe to pathological models of deafness.

On the other hand, university teaching based on the socio-cultural understanding of being deaf would espouse the view that some Deaf people, just like members of a distinct ethnic group, do not want to be like those with typical hearing because the abilities to speak and hear are not only unrealistic but also undesirable goals for them. Such teaching would embrace the view explained by Reagan (1995) that for Deaf students the appropriate comparison group is not individuals with physical, sensory, cognitive or other disabilities but members of other non-dominant cultural and linguistic groups such as the Hispanics in the United States. Teaching based on this mindset is therefore more likely to seek to know about and believe in Deaf learners' visual-gestural language and strengths which are construed as assets. Informed by the socio-cultural model, university teaching would perceive deafness as Deaf gain rather than hearing loss.

Teaching would therefore recognise the existence of Deaf epistemology, which Holcomb (2010) said relies heavily on personal testimonies, personal experiences and personal accounts to document knowledge. Universities may need to adopt deaf-centric policies shaped by Deaf epistemology in an effort to improve the academic performance of deaf students. Reliance on personal experiences in teaching is consistent with constructivist approaches in which Brown and Paatsch (2010) pointed out that much of the learning is opportunistic, authentic and "owned" by the learner. This is in tandem with what Garberoglio et al. (2012) called humanist teaching orientations in which there is a focus on the individual student and willingness to meet varying individual needs. Such orientations are the antithesis of teaching orientations of subordination in which students are viewed as subordinates in need of supervision. A socio-cultural understanding of deafness appears to be congruent with constructivist theories of teaching and learning characterised by humanist approaches. Such approaches are consistent with what Scheetz (2004) espoused as strategies involving communication, interaction and intervention based on respect, thoughtfulness, emotional integrity and authenticity.

In general, university education needs to do more to recognise the existence of multiple epistemologies for diverse learners. Multiple epistemologies suggest that individuals learn in different ways, shaped by life factors such as

Unyoking Deaf Culture from Disability   63

education, family, ethnicity, history and regional beliefs (Paul & Moores, 2010). With respect to deaf knowledge perspectives, Paul and Moores (2010) identified two major groups of deaf knowledge perspectives that are of interest here, namely the sociological and anthropological perspective as well as the historical/psychological and literary perspective.

In the sociological and anthropological knowledge perspective, there is the adoption of a naturalised, critical epistemological stance in evaluating research and the epistemology of a positive deaf identity; how personal epistemologies can help form deaf education policies; and valuing deaf indigenous knowledge in research. Deaf indigenous knowledge can be captured well by deaf researchers. Cooper (2012) observed that the idea that minority groups should be studied only by members of those groups potentially can be supported in two ways. First, there is the thought that members of the minority group are in an epistemically-privileged position: they have first-hand knowledge of what it is like to be a member of the group. Second, some theorists are inspired by the idea that knowledge is power and claim the right for minorities to study themselves as a political statement. However, Cooper (2012) rejected this view, pointing out that it is problematic, as in many cases one will be left with very few people who are "qualified" to study a way of being. She argued that when few people work on a problem, the chances of any of them being able to solve it are reduced. University departments therefore need to involve both hearing and Deaf researchers in research on deaf epistemologies.

In the historical/psychological and literary knowledge perspective, there is consideration of competing epistemologies in educating deaf learners and the benefit of reading literature with deaf characters for all students. The competing epistemologies in education generally, and in the education of deaf students specifically, need to be brought for explicit analysis. Analysis would reveal university curricula considerations that liberate, rather than domesticate, and those that celebrate diversity rather than assimilate. Approaches to teaching deaf learners that utilise oralism, total communication and sign-bilingualism need to be unemotionally analysed. The intention of a good university curriculum should be for decolonising rather than colonising others. Policy and practice on sign-bilingual education in universities would revolve principally around the use of sign language for those students for whom it is identified as the preferred language. Sign language would thus be recognised as a language of teaching, learning and examination. Decisions about linguistic support, access to the curriculum and relevant assessments should be based on strengths rather than perceived weaknesses of the deaf students. Tertiary level literature would also reflect diversity as natural and so should have diverse characters in various roles.

Conclusion

African universities have tended to unreflectively filter their understanding of the condition of being deaf through a Western-borrowed pathological model that views deafness as a disability in need of remediation. They have misled

64 Martin Musengi

themselves to believe that deaf people are, at least in a physiological sense, inferior to hearing people and they patronise deaf aspirants to university education. African universities have unthinkingly ignored their context of protest and struggle against colonialism which should make them front-runners in open-minded recognition and celebration of diversity. The African view of personhood espoused in Ubuntu needs to be fully capitalised on as universities grapple to accommodate disability, in general, and the condition of being deaf, in particular. African universities would, on the basis of Ubuntu, eschew the colonial view of deafness as a communication disability and thereby avoid attempting to assimilate deaf students into a dominant hearing culture. On the basis of the African view of personhood, university administrations are likely to reach the inescapable conclusion that at least some deaf students ought to be considered as culturally Deaf rather than deaf and disabled. Once such a conclusion is reached, Deaf epistemologies, among other diverse epistemologies, would give rise to humanist philosophies and practices that decolonise education for this group of students. Curricula considerations on these bases would enable inclusive African university education for liberation, rather than domestication; for celebrating diversity rather than assimilation; and for decolonising rather than colonising others. There is immense potential for African universities to provide decolonised, relevant and quality education in terms of cognitive justice not only for deaf students but also for the broad diversity of the student body.

Note

1 Throughout this chapter words directly from sign language are represented in capital letters to differentiate them from words from any spoken language, a practice that is called glossing.

References

American Psychological Association (APA). (2013). *Diagnostic and statistical manual of mental disorders DSM 5* (Vol. 5).

Andrews, J. F., Leigh, I. W., & Weiner, M. J. (2004). *Deaf people: Evolving perspectives from psychology, education and sociology*. Pearson.

Barnes, C. (1998). The social model of disability: A sociological phenomenon ignored by sociologists? In T. Shakespeare (Ed.), *Disability reader: Social science perspectives* (pp. 23–46). Continuum.

Barnes, C., & Mercer, G. (2005). *The social model of disability: Europe and the majority*. Disability Press.

Bauman, H-D. (2004). Audism: exploring the metaphysics of oppression. *Journal of Deaf Studies and Deaf Education, 9*(2), 240–246. https://doi.org/10.1093/deafed/enh025

Baumann, H. D. L., & Murray, J. M. (2009). Reframing: From hearing loss to deaf gain. *Deaf Studies Digital Journal, 1*(1), 1–10.

Bavelier, D., Dye, M. W. G., & Hauser, P. C. (2006). Do deaf individuals see better? *Trends in Cognitive Science, 10*, 512–518.

Unyoking Deaf Culture from Disability   65

Bellugi, U., O'Grady, L., Lillo-Martin, D., O'Grady, M., van Hoek, K., & Corina, D. (1990). Enhancement of spatial cognition in deaf children. In V. Volterra & C. Erting (Eds.), *From gesture to language in hearing and deaf children* (pp. 278–298). Springer.

Berghs, M., Chataika, T., El-Lahib, Y., & Dube, K. (2020). Introducing disability activism. In M. Berghs., T. Chataika., Y. El-Lahib, & K. Dube (Eds.), *The Routledge handbook of disability activism.* (pp. 3–20). Routledge.

Brown, P. M., & Paatsch, L. E. (2010). Beliefs, practices and expectations of oral teachers of the deaf. *Deafness & Education International, 12*(3), 135–148.

Camay, P. & Gordon, A. J. (Eds.). (1998). *Advocacy in Southern Africa: Lessons for the future.* Co-operative for Research and Education (CORE).

Charlton, J. I. (1998). *Nothing about us without us: Disability, oppression and empowerment.* University of California Press.

Cooper, R. (2012). Can it be a good thing to be deaf? In P. V. Paul & D. F. Moores (Eds.), *Deaf epistemologies: Multiple perspectives on the acquisition of knowledge.* (pp. 39–78). Gallaudet University Press.

Devlieger, P. J. (1998). Physical 'disability' in Bantu languages: Understanding the relativity of classification and meaning. *International Journal of Rehabilitation Research, 21*, 63–70.

Devlieger, P. J. (1999). Frames of reference in African proverbs on disability. *International Journal of Disability, Development and Education, 46*(4), 439–451.

Edwards, S., Makunga, N., Ngcobo, S., & Dhlomo, M. (2004). Ubuntu: A cultural method of mental health promotion. *International Journal of Mental Health Promotion, 6*(4), 17–22.

Emmorey, K., & Kosslyn, S. M. (1996). Enhanced image-generation abilities in deaf signers: A right-hemisphere effect. *Brain and Cognition, 32*, 28–44.

Feder, E. K. (2013). Power/knowledge. In D. Taylor (Ed.), *Michel Foucault: Key concepts.* (pp. 55–68). Acumen.

Flanagan, F. M. (2003). Teaching as a vocation? *Oideas, 50*, 79–123.

Foucault, M. (1979). *Discipline and punish: The birth of the prison* (A. Sheridan, Trans.). Vintage.

Foucault, M. (1990). *The history of sexuality volume 1: An introduction* (R. Hurley, Trans.). Vintage.

Garberoglio, C. L., Gobble, M. E., & Cawthorn, S. W. (2012). A national perspective on teachers' efficacy beliefs in deaf education. *Journal of Deaf Studies and Deaf Education 17*(3), 367–383.

Grover, C., & Soldatic, K. (2013). Neoliberal restructuring, disabled people and social (in)security in Australia and Britain. *Scandinavian Journal of Disability Research, 15*(3), 216–232.

Hauser, P. C., O'Hearn, A., McKee, M., Steider, A., & Thew, D. (2010). Deaf epistemology: Deafhood and deafness. *American Annals of the Deaf, 154*(5), 486–492.

Holcomb, T. K. (2010). Deaf epistemology: The deaf way of knowing, *American Annals of the Deaf, 154*(5), 471–478.

Humphries, T. (1977). Audism: The making of a word. Unpublished essay.

Iriarte, E. G., McConkey, R., & Gilligan, R. H. (2016). *Disability and human rights: Global perspectives.* Palgrave MacMillan.

Kabzems, V., & Chimedza, R. (2002). Development assistance: Disability and education in Southern Africa. *Disability & Society, 17*(2), 147–157.

Kaplan, D. (2013). The definition of disability: Perspective of the disability community. *World Institute on Disability.* www.peoplewho.org/debate/kaplan.htm

66 *Martin Musengi*

Ladd, P. (2003). *Understanding deaf culture: In search of deafhood*. Multilingual Matters.

Lane, H. (1999). *The mask of benevolence: Disabling the deaf community*. Knopf.

Lave, J., & Wenger, E. (1991). *Situated learning: Legitimate peripheral participation*. Cambridge University Press.

Mallory, B. L. (1992). *Changing beliefs about disability in developing countries: Historical factors and sociocultural variables*. Monograph. University of New Hampshire.

Manombe-Ncube, J. (2016). *Advocacy lessons from the disability movement: Experiences from Southern and Eastern Africa*. Butterworth.

Mbigi, L., & Maree, J. (1995). *Ubuntu: The spirit of African transformation management*. Sigma Press.

Mbiti, J. (1969). *African religions and philosophies*. Doubleday and Company.

Menkiti, I. A. (2007). On the normative conception of a person. In K. Wiredu (Ed.), *A companion to African philosophy* (pp. 324–331). Heinneman.

Miller, M. S. (2010). Epistemology and people who are deaf. *American Annals of the Deaf*, *154*(5), 479–485.

Mladenov, T. (2015) Neoliberalism, postsocialism, disability, *Disability & Society*, *30*(3), 445–459.

Munoz-Baell, I. M., & Ruiz, T. M. (2000). Empowering the deaf: Let the deaf be deaf. *Journal of Epidemiology and Community Health*, *54*, 40–44.

Ndlovu-Gatsheni, S. J. (2013). *Empire, global coloniality and African subjectivity*. Berghahn Books.

Ndlovu-Gatsheni, S. J. (2018). Foreword: On epistemicides, linguicides, inventions and standardisations. In T. Kamuella & F. Ndhlovu (Eds.), *Social and political history of Southern Africa's languages*. (pp. vii–ix). Palgrave Macmillan.

Nhundu, V. (1995). Education with production in Zimbabwe: In search of curriculum reforms for national development. Doctoral dissertation. University of Alberta, Edmonton.

O'Neill, Y. V. (2009). Understanding speechlessness: Pre-enlightenment views. In C. Storbeck (Ed.), *Foundations of deaf education: Educ 4001 (course reader)* (pp. 1–5). School of Education, University of the Witwatersrand.

Oliver, M. (2009). *Understanding disability: From theory to practice*. Palgrave Macmillan.

Padden, C., & Humphries, T. (1988). *Deaf in America: Voices from a culture*. Harvard University Press.

Paul, P. V., & Moores, D. F. (2010). *Deaf epistemologies: Multiple perspectives on the acquisition of knowledge*. Gallaudet University Press.

Peters, S., & Chimedza, R. (2000). Conscientisation and the cultural politics of education: A radical minority perspective. *Comparative Education Review*, *44*(3), 245–271.

Reagan, T. (1995). A sociocultural understanding of deafness: American sign language and the culture of deaf people. *International Journal of Intercultural Relations*, *19*(2), 239–251.

Rose, H. M. (1995). Apprehending deaf culture. *Journal of Applied Communication Research*, *23*, 156–162.

Sakellariou, D., & Rotarou, E. S. (2017). Access to healthcare for men and women with disabilities in the UK: Secondary analysis of cross-sectional data. *BMJ*:e016614. doi:10.1136/bmjopen-2017-016614

Scheetz, N. A. (2004). *Psychosocial aspects of deafness*. Pearson.

Siple, L. A. (1994). Cultural patterns of deaf people. *International Journal of Intercultural Relations, 18*(3), 345–367.

Soldatic, K. (2018). Surplusisity: Neo-liberalism and disability and precarity. In B. Watermeyer, J. McKenzie, & L. Swart (Eds.). *The Palgrave handbook of disability and citizenship in the global south* (pp. 13–26). Palgrave Macmillan.

Spivak, G. (1999). *A critique of postcolonial reason: Towards a history of the vanishing present.* Harvard University Press.

Stone, E. (2001). A complicated struggle: disability, survival and social change. In M. Priestley (Ed.), *Disability and the life course: Global perspectives.* (pp. 50–64). Cambridge University Press.

Torres, M. T. (1995). A postmodern perspective on the issue of deafness as culture versus pathology. *Journal of the American Deafness and Rehabilitation Association, 29*, 1–7.

United Nations Convention on the Rights of People with Disabilities (UNCRPD). (2006). *Convention on the rights of persons with disabilities and optional protocol.* United Nations.

United Nations Educational, Scientific and Cultural Organisation (UNESCO). (1994). *The Salamanca statement and framework for action on special needs education.* UNESCO.

wa Thiong'o, Ngũgĩ. (1986). *Decolonising the mind: The politics of language in African literature.* Heinemann Educational Books.

Weber, J. (2015). Negotiating deaf identity in an audist educational environment: An arts-based inquiry. *Ubiquity, The Journal of Literature, Literacy and Arts. Research Strand, 2*(2), 80–113.

Wenger, E. (1998). *Communities of practice: Learning, meaning and identity.* Cambridge University Press.

Wenger, E., McDermott, R., & Snyder, W. M. (2002). *Cultivating communities of practice.* Harvard Business Press.

Woodward, J. (1972). *How you gonna get to heaven if you can't talk with Jesus: On depathologising deafness.* TJ Publishers.

World Health Organisation (WHO). (1980). *International classification of impairments, disabilities, and handicaps: A manual of classification relating to the consequences of disease.* WHO.

World Health Organisation. (2002). *International classification of functioning, disability and health.* WHO.

World Health Organisation. (2014). *ICD-10-CM official guidelines for coding and reporting* (10th ed.). WHO.

6 Theorising Feminist Voices in the Curriculum in an African University

Beatrice Akala

Introducing a Case of Missing Voices in an African University Curriculum

The African university is in the vanguard of knowledge production and dissemination, besides being a hub of skills development and innovation. As such, most nations across the continent have aligned and juxtaposed their developmental goals, visions, and national plans to the goals of higher education. This is evident in Kenya's Vision 2030, a platform geared towards catapulting the nation to greater heights of industrialisation and technological development. South Africa's post-1994 transformation trajectory goals have also been aligned to those of higher education (Department of Education [DoE], White Paper, 1997; DoE, National Plan, 2001; Ellis, 2007; Mugo et al., 2015). However, cases of inequitable participation and representation in the academy have stifled the progression of the post-colonial African university. The minimal participation and representation and subsequent exclusion of women in particular has been of concern for feminists (Afonja, 2005; Collins, 1991, 2003; Mama, 2006). Their disenfranchisement has been heightened through persistent colonialist theorisation of knowledge and knowing, the gendered and exclusionary nature of knowledge production, and the lack of concrete representation of their experiences in the curriculum; for they are only passively implied in the curriculum (Asher, 2009; Coetzee, 2017; Collins, 1991).

A review of African universities, seen as ivory towers, depict them as exclusive spaces where the voices and experiences of the minority groups have been overshadowed by hegemonies (Mamdani, 2008; Mazrui, 1978). Knowledge production and a misrepresentation of feminist voices in the curriculum has hindered equitable recognition of women's abilities in advancing scholarship and laying a claim to knowledge and knowing (Collins, 2003). Feminist theorists have linked the alleged marginalisation of women in the academy to factors related to intersectionality, male dominance, and skewed power relations (Crenshaw, 1991, 2001). Often, which should not be the case, the voices of White middle-class women have carried more credence than those of minority groups (Mignolo, 2000; Oyewumi, 2003). Coetzee (2017) indicates that we should be concerned about who is rendered inaudible and invisible in the dominant processes and sites of Sub-Saharan knowledge

DOI: 10.4324/9781003228233-6

Theorising Feminist Voices in Curriculum   69

production. In their fight for inclusion, feminists have considered the absence of voice and other injustices in advocating equal opportunities in knowledge production and the emasculation of the curriculum and learning sites in order to disrupt the status quo (Collins, 1991; Icaza Garza, 2018).

Whereas White women have had a stable presence in the politics of knowledge, the voices of Black and African women have been absent. It is against this background that it is being argued that the reality of including feminist voices in the curriculum must be based on heterogeneity and not a selected group of women. Thus, the anomaly of normalising and using the views of White females as a representative of other groups has been contested (Collins, 2003). For instance, the predominance of images of White women in engineering reinforces and internalises stereotypes about Black women's inability and underachievement on the one hand, and the brilliance of White women in this field on the other (Nix & Perez-Felkner, 2019). As a riposte, the Black/African feminism movement in scholarship emerged as an alternative avenue of ameliorating Black women's position in the knowledge economy. Succinct perspectives of Black and African women's experiences and realities are being appropriated through this strand of feminism (Atanga, 2018; Beoku-Betts & Njambi, 2005; Coetzee, 2017; Oyewumi, 2003).

Whilst literature suggests that although race is the organising principle in colonial and post-colonial discourses, gendering is experienced differently. This is why critiquing the inclusion of and normalisation of Western middle-class voices at the expense of Black/African and ethnic minorities is an area of concern to decoloniality scholars (Asher, 2009; Collins, 2003). At the same time, Collins (2003, p. 47) refutes the perception that Black females' contributions to knowledge are inferior to those of the elite White males and their representatives who control and validate knowledge. Collins' cognition has therefore given latitude to the often distorted and excluded fluidity of Black women's experiences in homes, workplaces, political and sexual activism from mainstream, conservative and traditional discourses. The distortion ignores the interconnectedness between content and context (Atanga, 2018; Oyewumi, 2003).

Collins (2009) identifies omission, trivialisation, and depoliticisation as the main kinds of suppressions that feminists' thought, and scholarship is subjected to. Collins' exposure is aimed at legitimising Black feminist thought, centring their knowing and knowledge, and moving their lived experiences to the centre of knowledge. This theorisation marks a tremendous shift for Black women since they will not be just implied in a passive manner, but now they will be involved in an active manner (Collins, 2003; Dotson, 2015). Likewise, Mirza (2014) expands on this by stating that the normalisation of Whiteness has contributed to the distortion of the ontological experiences of Black, ethicised, and diasporic women. The erasure or hiding of powerful accounts of Black and ethicised women's suffrage denies them a place in White establishments such as universities. Black feminist analysis is more inclined towards reclaiming their (Black and ethnised) place in history and higher education.

70   *Beatrice Akala*

Decoloniality scholars and researchers seek to address the colonial knowledge structures that exclude the experiences of the marginalised and indigenous populations in general (Coetzee, 2017; Collins, 2003; Mama, 2011; Ndlovu-Gatsheni, 2016). They challenge the "othered" hierarchies of knowledge that are perpetuated through Western—non-Western binaries and discourses (Gaston Gayles & Smith, 2018; Manion & Shah, 2019; Sparks, 2017). Schiwy (2007) argues that the discourse of decolonisation has not appropriated gender subjectivity appropriately as its inclusion in discourses is often seen as an after-thought. On the other hand, decoloniality has taken cognisance of the economic, political, globalisation, epistemic, and racial aspects of colonialism whilst subverting the inclusion of gender. Not integrating gender in the current discourse is flawed and it eliminates and misappropriates the intersectionality of gender with class, race, sex, ethnicity, and religion. The subjectivities and positionality that occur during and as a result of the intersectionality must be accounted for in decoloniality debates and theorisation (Beoku-Betts & Njambi, 2005; Morley, 2006; Oyewumi, 2003). Consequently, feminists are against the fallacy of presenting knowledge as neutral and objective. It obliterates the fact that knowledge is entrenched in masculinities and the violent project of colonialism (De Jong et al., 2018).

According to Mohanty (2003a), the way we set a curriculum and the pedagogies we use to teach it tell(s) a story or stories. Not including women in the curriculum means their stories are not told, in Mohanty's version. In the case of Grande (2003), indigenous knowledges are often viewed as childish fiction or new age spiritualism. Sleeter (2010) agrees with Schiwy (2007) in observing that teaching a decolonised curriculum should problematise and re-order power relations and engender new habits, expectations, and the conceptualisation of appropriateness. It also requires rethinking the kinds of knowledge we encounter and the embedded worldviews. Schiwy (2007) is convinced that more deep connections need to be formed with regard to how knowledge intersects with the female body. Schiwy concludes that social memory and subalternised knowledge is embodied and transmitted in gendered ways (Schiwy, 2007, p. 272).

Theorising Feminisms and Key Arguments on Subjectivities

Feminist standpoint theory took root in the 1970s and 1980s, its core concern being the production of knowledge and the unfair practices of power. The theory in its vastness has addressed a myriad of issues that border on suppression and oppression (Harding, 1990, 2004). Despite the different kinds of feminisms that have arisen over time, it is clear that feminists' work is aimed at achieving a single goal, women's liberation (Edwards & Usher, 2002; Usher, 1996). The different waves of feminisms deal with the origin and teleology of gender inequality, misrecognition of women's contributions in public affairs and private spaces and the general devaluation and disenfranchisement of women (Fraser, 2005; Usher, 1996). Connell (2005) maintains that, as much as there are many feminisms and femininities, so there are masculinities

Theorising Feminist Voices in Curriculum   71

that are created, sustained, and mediated by history, race, class, sex, and culture. Freedman (2001, p. 2) describes a *feminist* as one who is interested in studying gender, understanding the cultural systems and signs that undergird the meanings assigned to sexually dimorphic bodies. Mama (in Salo, 2001) believes that feminism is a positive movement which is defined by its refusal to conform to any form of oppression advanced against women. The movement is committed to the alleviation of all forms of marginalisation encountered by women at all levels: internal, external, emotional, psychological, philosophical, social, economic, and political spheres. Farganis (1994, p. 15) views feminism as an Ideology or 'belief system', "an integrated set of theoretical assumptions that, taken together, structure a worldview that its adherents take to be true". Essentially, ideologies become problematic if they generatively erode the way people relate to each other. For instance, an ideology that celebrates masculinity and undermines femininity affects how women are treated and valued by society (Martin, 2008).

Weedon (1987) and Wodak (Wodak, 1997) share a common understanding with social constructivists in stating that different forms of subjectivities are intricately produced historically and that they shift depending on the discursive frames within which they are constituted. For this reason, a woman has to adjust and negotiate competing discourses that produce conflicting subject positions, her sense of self and her worldview. It is true that a woman who has to navigate and adjust to her dual roles of motherhood and wife, as framed, and informed through feminist thought on the one hand, and a working woman who is governed by the discourses of professionalism and masculinity, undergoes several contradictions. This particular individual is always experiencing conflicting and conflating states of *being* that she has to make meaning of through tactful negotiations. Weedon (1987) defines subjectivity as: "the conscious and unconscious thoughts and emotions of the individual, their sense of self and ways of understanding their relation to the world" (p. 32).

The universalisation and homogenisation of women's experiences has been an area of discord (Atanga, 2018; Oyewumi, 2003). Taking cognisance of this fact means that although women share a sisterhood, their conditions and experiences are divergent. In this regard, Oyeronke Oyewumi (2003) maintains that African feminism is disadvantaged because the views and ideologies that are promoted by the majority of feminists are from Western feminisms (Mohanty, 2003a). Oyeronke Oyewumi (2003) and Atanga (2013) opine that the poor portrayal and inadequate articulation of African women's troubles in Western feminists' scholarly work has to be amended. Nussbaum (1999) explicates that applying Western values indiscriminately to communities that cannot identify with them is an injustice (MacKinnon, 1993; Young, 1990). Mohanty's essay, *Under the Western Eye* (Mohanty, 1988) provides a critique of Western feminism on Third world women's experiences and struggles through a colonising discursive formation (Mohanty, 2003a). The essay elucidates on the power knowledge nexus, and how different cultural formations across feminisms have been undermined. It is inexplicable that the universalisation of knowledge through Eurocentrism and

72   Beatrice Akala

Western feminism has contributed to falsehoods regarding the inferiority of other cultures (Coetzee, 2017).

The gender binary also entrenches gender inequalities because of its narrow conceptualisation of gender and sex (Schiwy, 2007). Essentialising gender assumes mutual exclusivity of the gender/sex binary which leads to a false apprehension and a distorted version of the experiences and circumstances of the "other". I argue that privilege breeds and nurtures blindness to those who do not enjoy similar privileges. It also conceals hierarchical power relations and protects the interests of the minority ruling class. The experiences of Black women who are subjected to simultaneous interlocking and multiple subordinations that are related to race, class, gender, culture, and sexual orientation cannot be captured fully in a single framework (Crenshaw, 2001). A single framework does not consider the material complexity, reality, and agency of Third World women's bodies. The all-hands-on-deck strategy can dislodge the single narrative matrix (Mohanty, 1998).

Butler (1990) advocates for the voices of women who feel left out of the conventional and normalised categories. These categories rarely represent the core of their being that is interlinked and permeated with other identities such as race, ethnicity, class, age, and sexuality-intersectionality. Likewise, Oyeronke Oyewumi's views regarding feminism and how African feminisms have been sidelined are articulated in the excerpt below:

> The term feminism usually refers to historically recent European and American social movements founded to struggle for female equality. … the term feminist has a broader reach … it describes a range of behaviour indicating female agency and self-determination … Filomena Africa … wrote about Africa as the original home of feminist principles. In this sense, then, African feminism is a tautology.
>
> (Oyewumi, 2003, pp. 1–2)

African feminism prioritises gender inequalities that are catapulted through the changing political, economic, social, spatial, religious, and cultural landscape on the African continent. This strand of feminism tacitly sensitises women to question and redefine the superimposed gender roles (Jacobs, 2013). As iterated, centring women's experiences on middle-class Western women is flawed, and it has omitted the stories of African women, or given a version that jeopardises their contexts and lived realities. As a matter of fact, the realities of women on the African continent are as diverse as there are cultures, ethnic groups, languages, religious affiliations, races, colonial experiences, sovereignty of nations, and traditions. This means that, as a complex group, they cannot fit into a utopian narrative (Kolawole, 2002). However, Mama (in Salo, 2001) thinks that the problems with Western feminisms are miniature in comparison to White domination of global politics and global capitalism. According to Mama (2011), it is possible that Western feminisms have listened to the concerns that were raised by Black and African feminists regarding the varied experiences of racism and the simplistic theorisation of gender.

Theorising Feminist Voices in Curriculum   73

More complex theories, like post-colonialism feminist theory, have emerged and encapsulated class, race, culture, and gender relations as clusters of analysis, according to Mama (in Salo, 2001) and Asher (2009). The convergence of the several feminisms has culminated in curating a transformative agenda, and championing for meaningful change and acknowledgement of women's lived experiences (Basow, 1992; Lindsey & Christie, 1997). Pursuant to discourses of gender inequalities and inequities that have been advanced by gender construction theorists, similar elucidations on gender can be derived from feminist theorisation. As far as education is concerned, radical feminists put up a more nuanced argument that a generalisation of knowledge claims is adversarial because knowledge is contextual. As such, knowledge cannot be extricated from one's daily experiences. This disconnect is contrary to the "straitjacket of the masculine paradigm" that obscures how non-academic factors affect the learning experience of women" (Farganis, 1994, p. 40; Henry, 2005). The same view is shared by post-structuralism in advancing the view that knowledge and truth claims are contextual and relative (Foucault, 1994). Overall, feminist research and epistemologies are aimed at producing knowledge and contributing towards empowering women; releasing their voices, transforming structures and creating more opportunities for equal participation, representation and access (Asher, 2009; Harding, 1990; Lindsey & Christie, 1997, p. 13).

Redefining the African University through Curriculum Reforms

The status of the African university post-colonialism has been explained as increasingly coming under scrutiny. Fierce debates across the continent have culminated in the view that although the gains of political liberation have been widely celebrated, the African university has not gained epistemic and academic liberation (Mamdani, 2008; Mazrui, 1978; Mbembe, 2017; Ndlovu-Gatsheni, 2016; wa Thiong'o, 1992). The African university is still under the yoke of colonialism years after most the countries have gained political independence. It is largely advancing Eurocentrism in its academic and scholarship engagements. It is undoubtable that knowledge and the content of the curriculum in African universities has been based on a singularity of Eurocentrism (Ndlovu-Gatsheni, 2016; wa Thiong'o, 1992). This has resulted in the relegation of indigenous knowledges to the peripheries, which has been generally detrimental to the African knowledge systems. They have been positioned as myth and inferior to Western logic and knowledges (Dei, 2007; Hountondji, 1996).

A curriculum is a powerful tool through which the marginalised groups can challenge systems of oppression. Hence, African universities have embarked on curriculum reforms that are focused on achieving inclusivity in representation in knowledge production and dissemination, reclaiming indigenous knowledges from the margins. Consequently, current debates are linked to addressing the question of relevance of selected curriculum content and knowledge to the African situation (Mama, 2006; Ndlovu-Gatsheni,

2016; wa Thiong'o, 1992). Dislocating Western knowledges that have been centred around the views and theories of White middle-class men with more Afrocentric and progressive theorisations is a major focus and goal of decolonising the curriculum (Fanon, 2007; Hountondji, 1996; wa Thiong'o, 1992). However, curriculum content for an African university is also contestable. Whereas some scholars have argued that an African epistemology should be centred in the curriculum and other knowledges should be included on the basis of their relevance (Dei, 2007; Ndlovu-Gatsheni, 2016; wa Thiong'o, 1992), those of contrasting opinion have contended that an African university cannot exist in isolation. They have therefore suggested a hybridisation of the curriculum that amalgamates Afrocentrism and Eurocentrism in conceptualising the ideal curriculum for the continent (Achebe, 2009).

Asher (2009) intimates that transculturality is a reality in former colonial territories. Based on Asher's understanding, it is therefore apparent that the notion of a curriculum being a neutral document is implausible. Lovet and Smith (1995) argue that the process of selecting what goes into the curriculum is undergirded by power relationships of the dominant groups and minorities. Thus, what is selected in terms of knowledge, values, and skills is layered with racial, gender, social class, and sexual biases. The biases are encoded in disciplinary knowledge that is taught in classrooms. This is in spite of a curriculum being characterised by the vision of creating a good society and a good life for the learners and citizens. This calls for a reflection on the content and the values that the young people are exposed to, and to whether what is taught enables or disempowers them to make moral judgements that they can identify with. We need to ask and be concerned about whether the curriculum reflects the truth regarding values, belief, nature, and the good life and future we envision for the young people (Sleeter, 2010).

Decolonisation debates should be broadened to include a myriad of factors that have exacerbated exclusion in an African university. Asher (2009) explains that forces of capitalism and globalisation are intricately linked to colonialism. Furthermore, Asher (2009) states that non-Western voices have been silenced and regulated by market forces. Fanon (2007) opines that racism should be a key factor in decoloniality because of its role as an organising principle in settler and post-colonial societies. As a consequence, this has resulted in yoking of ethnic and racial minorities through capitalism, racism, and cross-cultural ethnic relations. It is undeniable that race and class intersect; they co-constitute each other through processes of differentiation that form barriers between rich/poor, male/female, White/Black/people of colour (Kane, 2007). The relegation to the margins has led to the thriving of postcolonial discourses and yet they are limited in their conceptualisation of the neocolonial condition in African universities (Dei, 2007; Fanon, 2007, 2008; Hountondji, 1996; Mbembe, 2017; wa Thiong'o, 1992).

Nyamnjoh (2019) has contended that, for African universities to have relevance to their contexts, they have to look beyond the academy and embrace everyday wisdoms and insights from ordinary African people. Examples can also be drawn from the decolonisation discourse across South African

Theorising Feminist Voices in Curriculum 75

campuses that has gone beyond epistemological access and staff composition, and now includes challenges to the exclusivity of spaces, university cultures and traditions and skewed histories (Ajani, 2019; Calitz, 2018). Another point to observe is the overlapping and intertwining between coloniser and colonised identities, and how the overlapping subsequently constructs oppressive subjectivities and hierarchies in schools, society, curriculum, and teaching (Asher, 2009; Kane, 2007). Mignolo (2003) argues that the coloniality of any nature; power, knowledge, being, capitalism, and gender constitutes an epistemic location where reality is conceived and experienced. Besides, the dominant locale of enunciation where an individual interacts with humans and non-humans is hierarchical and often violent. This is why those whose voices are excluded in the curriculum are susceptible to symbolic violence as they encounter institutional environments that are hostile to their difference (Fanon, 2007, 2008; Mignolo, 2003).

Engaging Feminists' Voices in Decolonising the Curriculum

Black feminists believe that epistemic justice can be achieved through challenging hegemonies, pedagogies of positionality, geographical and historical situatedness, plurality, reflexivity, relationality, and transition. The encounter between feminisms and coloniality uses Black and decolonial feminist ideas in disrupting normalised knowledges and teaching approaches that reproduce the status quo. This approach instead recasts the gaze in recognising difference as the pivotal point of knowledge (Bhambra et al., 2018; Icaza Garza & Vázquez, 2018; Kolawole, 2002). Gaztambide-Fernández (2012) argues that decolonisation is plausible through the pedagogy of solidarity that encapsulates the inscription of colonial logics and legacies that ensure the perpetuation of colonialism.

The pedagogy of solidarity is composed of three elements: relational (acknowledging the complexities within individual histories and lived realities); transitive (contingency/transient consensus about what attitudes are normal/practices that are just/unjust); and the creative, which is concerned with the multiplicity of cultural solidarity. Gaztambide-Fernández (2012) explicates that the three elements have the ability to restore human relations and humanity amongst colonised people. Coetzee avers that Western feminism occupies a unique epistemological position that is rich in resources to subvert, rupture, and enrich these dominant systems of knowledge (Coetzee, 2017; Oyewumi, 2003).

Institutionalised decolonisation cannot be pre-determined, it has to respond to the realities and needs of the people. Reconciliation and forgiveness should be part of the decolonisation trajectory (Gaztambide-Fernández, 2012). Under the prism of feminist solidarity strategy, the local and global are conceived as existing simultaneously and they constitute each other; they are not confined to geography or territory (Atanga, 2018; Mama, 2011; Oyewumi, 2003). The relationship between local and global is foregrounded, while the links are conceptual, material, temporal, and universal/specific. The

76 Beatrice Akala

directionality of power is also included in the framework of analysis (Collins, 2003; Mohanty, 2003a). Mohanty explains that Western feminists should join Third World feminists in their struggles on account of shared solidarity (Coetzee, 2017; Mohanty, 2003a). To avoid universalisation and the undermining of women's lived experiences, cross-cultural/transnational feminists should take cognisance of the micropolitical of context, subjectivities, realities, and struggles (Kolawole, 2002; Mohanty, 2003a). Crucially, Mohanty's concern is how we can find a balance between the local and global without perpetuating relativism through the North/South binaries.

This means paying attention regarding what it would mean to be attentive to the micropolitics of everyday life as well as to the larger processes that recolonise the culture and identities of people across the globe. How we think of the local and of the global and vice versa without falling into colonising or cultural relativist platitudes about difference is also crucial in this intellectual and political landscape. And for Mohanty, this kind of thinking is tied to a revised race-and-gender-conscious historical materialism (Mohanty, 2003a, p. 509).

A methodology that conceptualises and references materialism in cross-cultural studies and Third World countries that are rebutting recolonisation have the ability to promote a paradigm for inclusivity and social justice (Mama, 2006, 201]; Mohanty, 2003b). In choosing how and why a curriculum should be local or global, it is imperative to think about the importance of the scholarship being advanced in relation to knowledge and citizenship struggles. Recognising that decolonisation rests in separate locales that are linked to human struggles (intersectionality) averts being implicated in colonisation and being othered in discourses of knowledge production and dissemination. The panacea requires involvement from all stakeholders; interstices of race, gender, culture, and nation are context specific (Asher, 2005; Fanon, 2007; Kane, 2007).

Unlearning repression through engaging ourselves and our psychic aspects of the self has been suggested by Mohanty (1989). However, Arvin et al. (2013) argue that settler colonialism was and continues to be a gendered space. Women's academic participation is intricately linked to indigenous people's dispossession and colonialisation. An understanding of how heteropatriarchy and settler colonialism intersect will provide a better understanding of how women have been kept on the periphery of knowledge production and dissemination in the academy. This means that other nuanced Black/African and ethnic experiences ought to be incorporated into feminism scholarship other than those of White Western feminism (Crenshaw, 1991, 2001; Sabzalian, 2018). Nxumalo and Cedillo (2017) identify the absence of Black feminism geographies, indigenous onto-epistemologies, and spatial relevance in mainstream early childhood research and practice. Due to the absence and extraordinary mismatch, the centring and imposition of the dominance of Eurocentrism and Western knowledge is maintained. The two authors invite a conversation between Black feminists, indigenous onto-epistemologies, and post-humanists in order to disrupt anthropocentric narratives of "knowing a

Theorising Feminist Voices in Curriculum   77

place" whilst exposing the complexities in humanity. Similarly, according to Sabzalian (2018), native feminists give a radical account of land, life, and the future, with the aim of bringing about decolonial knowledges and futures. This approach works towards advancing inclusivity in justice programmes by entrenching history and context.

Feminists can also benefit from the ideas championed by Dei (2018) as he writes of a solidarity that ought to transcend the current framing based on the binary of Black/African people, which is based on Blackness/skin colour or territorial/geographical positioning/occupation of Black/African people. According to Dei, embracing multiple perspectives of Blackness/Africanness is likely to solve the current stalemate on indigeneity and decolonisation. The multiplicity and plurality of perspectives must be rooted in indigeneity, which is a departure from an Africanness or Blackness that is rooted in Euro-American culture and knowledge traditions. The paradigm shift will appropriate Black/Africa and diasporic communities' realities, histories, experiences, culture, and identities regardless of geographical location through the appropriate analytic frames and discursive formations and authority (Atanga, 2018; Oyewumi, 2003). Dei and Black/African feminists advocate for a resistance of the captivity of colonial experience and the entrapment of the academy by offering new ways of education and schooling even though the views may be divergent due to the heterogeneity in the Black/African people (Dei, 2018, p. 136; Kolawole, 2002; Oyewumi, 2003).

Sabzalian (2018) argues that in order for a curricular standpoint to be effective politically and pedagogically, it has to be true to its feminist roots and native feminist critique. Native feminist theories account for the experiences, knowledge, and lands of indigenous people and their decolonial struggles. Sabzalian (2018) unequivocally states that "Native feminist theories must go wherever feminist and curricular standpoint theories go. If not, they are not" (Sabzalian, 2018, p. 376). In addition, native feminist theorisation has the ability to develop new capabilities that can be used to counter colonial logic. Schiwy (2007) and Mama (2011) argue that since femininity and masculinity are colonial constructs, discourses of indigeneity have to include gender complementarity as a way of thinking about decoloniality and undoing of colonial legacies. According to Khader (2018), the interest in the Global South is in relation to constructs that do not challenge Western imperialism domination.

Mohanty (2003b) chooses to support a feminism praxis that is borderless in entrenching decoloniality. Feminism without borders is not limited by race, nationality, sexuality, culture, social class, or religion. According to Mohanty, social justice must be advanced through transnationality because it transcends the demarcations created by colonial borders that obfuscate injustices (Khader, 2018; McLaren, 2017). A similar view has been expressed by Woodhull's (1993) theorisation of decolonisation of space in North African and Maghreb literature as being plural, where body and language, masculinity and femininity, voice and writing, native and foreign languages, marginalised and hegemonic cultures intermingle freely without merging to form a

78   Beatrice Akala

new unity. By using the Algerian context, Lazreg (2005) argues that the Western scientists, ethnologists, and anthropologists have failed to account for the differences in women is post-colonial colonies. Thus, the dilemma in homogenising women fuels biases embedded in the objectification of "different" which is presented as the unmediated "other", the embodiments of cultures presumed inferior and classified as "traditional" or "patriarchal" (Lazreg, 2005, p. 68).

According to Schiwy (2007), the dichotomy of gender complementarity in decolonisation is not only important in discourses of colonial power, but also in highlighting the need for inclusivity and mutual existence of all traditions in epistemologies, however temporal the relationship might be. When gender complementarity serves as an ideal for imagining decolonised epistemic relations with the West, the colonial subalternisation of knowledge, perspectives, genealogies, and technologies of the intellect gives way to a fruitful coexistence where all traditions shed light on each other (Schiwy, 2007, p. 287). The disciplinary space in the university has also been identified as a place of struggle. It is seen as an isle that not only advances disciplinary knowledge but is also an exclusionary space that promotes monolithic canons of knowledge, structures, and cultures (Ajani, 2019; Coetzee, 2017; Mamdani, 2008). Such spaces should adopt trans- and interdisciplinary approaches for inclusivity in order to destabilise colonialism and male dominance, and to nourish critical thought in universities to destabilise colonial and dominance in university, nourish critical thought and dismantle male-dominated and power implications (Parker et al., 2017). Nadar (2014) asserts that narrative/knowing is a feature of African feminist epistemology and research that is important because stories encourage and encompass suspicion of master/grand narratives of knowledge, objection to objectivity, reflexivity to positioning of researchers; they centre transformation and change. Their main aim is posing an objection to conventional ways of knowing, including an interrogation of scientific thought. Icaza Garza (2018) suggests that in order to overcome the coloniality of gender, we have to unlearn privileges (race, epistemic, socio-economic) and re-learn from communal forms of resistance.

Collins (2009) finally proposes an alternative in Afrocentric feminist epistemology as a conduit of appropriating the experiences of minority groups and overcoming decoupling colonial theorisations. The alternative is indicative of how knowledge is created and the role it plays in fostering resistance. Collins' (2009) criteria for Black feminist epistemology encompasses the following:

1. A criterion on meaning, which takes lived experience and "practical images" as important for grounding and making knowledge claims;
2. A criterion for assessment, which refers to vetting knowledge through dialogue with and among one's community/communities;
3. A criterion for members of one's community/communities, which articulates forms of competence required for members of a given community of knowers;

4. A criterion on knower adequacy, which stipulates that those making claims to knowledge need to also have moral or ethical connections to those claims.

Collins' creation of knowledge criteria can be summarised into two key tenets. Criteria 2 and 3 are concerned with knowledge production, whereas 1 and 4 deal with knowledge possession (Dotson, 2015). I believe that some of the questions that are being debated by decolonial scholars can be located in Collins' tenets. Questions of whose knowledge, context, space, and relevance are well within the summaries provided by Dotson (2015). In conclusion, I note that emancipation of the curriculum must take cognisance of the intersectionality of gender, class, and race/ethnicity/sexual orientation/ableness. This is very important for social justice, research, teaching, and praxis because it conceptualises how people experience inclusion, exclusion, and marginalisation by providing several perspectives as opposed to a single universalised narrative (Icaza Garza & Icaza Garza & Vázquez, 2017).

Concluding Remarks

This chapter has appropriated and recognised the marginalisation that female voices have encountered in an African university and beyond. It is clear that in order for decolonisation to be a reality in an African university, the colonial gaze has to be readjusted in order to have a clear understanding and view of how different subjectivities such as gender have been constructed and sustained in knowledge production and dissemination. The quandary of hegemonic power that is structural, disempowers epistemologically because it defines knowledge and knowing from which the marginalised communities and their experiences are excluded (Dotson, 2015). This is why Collins (2003) argues that the subjugation of Black women's experiences and knowledge in traditional genres has led them to reimagine alternative ways of producing and validating their own knowledge. Genres such as music, art, literature, and everyday conversations are increasingly becoming popular channels of producing and disseminating knowledge in minority and ethnic groups. The idea of epistemic solidarity is also very convincing; Black/African feminists cannot regain and reclaim their positions in an African university if they do not find support from dominant and minority groups alike (Dei, 2018; Gaztambide-Fernández, 2012; Mama, 2011; Mohanty, 2003b). Finally, I argue that in order to avoid universalisation of women's experiences, intersectionality has to be at the core of discourses of decolonising the curriculum in an African university. This will ensure epistemic and ontological justice.

References

Achebe, C. (2009). *The education of a British-protected child: Essays*. Penguin Group.
Afonja, S. (2005). *Gender and feminism in African development discourse*. Indiana University: Institute for Advanced Study.

80 *Beatrice Akala*

Ajani, O. A. (2019). Decolonisation of education in African contexts. *African Renaissance, 16*(2), 101–120.

Akala, B. (2019). Intersecting human development, social justice and gender equity: A capability option. *Education as Change, 23*(1), 1–22.

Arvin, M., Tuck, E., & Morrill, A. (2013). Decolonizing feminism: Challenging connections between settler colonialism and heteropatriarchy. *Feminist Formations*, 8–34.

Asher, N. (2005). At the interstices: Engaging postcolonial and feminist perspectives for a multicultural education pedagogy in the South. *Teachers College Record, 107*(5), 1079–1106.

Asher, N. (2009). Decolonizing curriculum. In *Curriculum studies handbook: The next moment*, (p. 393). Routledge.

Atanga, L. L. (2013). African feminism? In *Gender and language in Sub-Saharan Africa: Tradition, struggle, and change* (pp. 301–314). doi:10.1075/impact.33.20ata

Atanga, L. L. (2018). A gender inclusive university governance: An analysis of the University of Bamenda. MBA Dissertation. University of Bamenda.

Basow, S. A. (1992). *Gender: Stereotypes and roles.* Thomson Brooks/Cole Publishing Co.

Beoku-Betts, J., & Njambi, W. N. (2005). African feminist scholars in women's studies: Negotiating spaces of dislocation and transformation in the study of women. *Meridians, 6*(1), 113–132.

Bhambra, G. K., Gebrial, D., & Nişancıoğlu, K. (2018). *Decolonising the university.* Pluto Press.

Butler, J. (1990). *Gender trouble: Feminism and the subversion of identity.* Routledge.

Calitz, T. (2018). Recognition as reparation: A participatory approach to (mis)recognition and decolonisation in South African higher education. *Educational Research for Social Change, 7*(SPE), 46–59.

Coetzee, A. A. (2017). African feminism as decolonising force: A philosophical exploration of the work of Oyeronke Oyewumi. Doctoral dissertation. Stellenbosch University.

Collins, P. H. (1991). On our own terms: Self-defined standpoints and curriculum transformation. *National Women's Studies Association (NWSA) Journal, 3*(3), 367–381.

Collins, P. H. (2003). Toward an Afrocentric feminist epistemology. In Y. S. Lincoln & N. K. Denzin (Eds.). *Turning points in qualitative research: Tying knots in a handkerchief* (pp. 47–72). AltaMira Press.

Collins, P. H. (2009). *Black feminist thought: Knowledge, consciousness, and the politics of empowerment.* Routledge Classics.

Connell, R. W. (2005). Change among the gatekeepers: Men, masculinities, and gender equality in the global arena. *Signs: Journal of Women in Culture and Society, 30*(3), 1801–1825.

Crenshaw, K. (1991). Mapping the margins: Intersectionality, identity politics, and violence against women of color. *Stanford Law Review, 43*(6), 1241–1299.

Crenshaw, K. (2001, September). The intersectionality of gender and race discrimination. In *World conference against racism, racial discrimination, xenophobia and related intolerance.* Durban, South Africa.

De Jong, S., Icaza, R., & Rutazibwa, O. U. (Eds.). (2018). *Decolonization and feminisms in global teaching and learning.* Routledge.

Dei, G. J. S. (2007). The denial of difference: Reframing anti-racist praxis. *Race and racialization: Essential readings*, 188–198.

Theorising Feminist Voices in Curriculum 81

Dei, G. J. S. (2018). "Black like me": Reframing blackness for decolonial politics. *Educational Studies*, *54*(2), 117–142.

Department of Education. (1997). *A programme for the transformation of higher education* [White paper]. Pretoria.

Department of Education. (2001). National plan for higher education. *Government Gazette*. (No. 22138, Notice 230).

Dotson, K. (2015). Inheriting Patricia Hill Collins's black feminist epistemology. *Ethnic and Racial Studies*, *38*(13), 2322–2328.

Edwards, R., & Usher, R. (2002). *Postmodernism and education: Different voices, different worlds*. Routledge.

Ellis, A. (2007). *Gender and economic growth in Kenya: Unleashing the power of women*. World Bank Publications.

Fanon, F. (2007). *The wretched of the earth*. Grove/Atlantic, Inc.

Fanon, F. (2008). *Black skin, white masks*. Grove Press.

Farganis, S. (1994). *Situating feminism: From thought to action* (Vol. 2). SAGE Publications.

Foucault, M. (1994). Psychiatric power. In P. Rabinow (Ed.), *Ethics: Subjectivity and truth* (pp. 39–50). The New Press.

Fraser, N. (2005). *Reframing justice*. Uitgeverij Van Gorcum.

Freedman, J. (2001). *Concepts in the social sciences: Feminism*. Open University.

Gaston Gayles, J., & Smith, K. N. (2018). Advancing theoretical frameworks for intersectional research on women in STEM. *New Directions for Institutional Research*, *2018*(179), 27–43.

Gaztambide-Fernández, R. A. (2012). Decolonization and the pedagogy of Solidarity. *Decolonization: Indigeneity, Education and Society*, *1*(1), 41–67.

Grande, S. (2003). Whitestream feminism and the colonialist project: A review of contemporary feminist pedagogy and praxis. *Educational Theory*, *53*(3), 329–346.

Harding, S. (1990). Feminism and theories of scientific knowledge. *Women: A Cultural Review*, *1*(1), 87–98.

Harding, S. G. (Ed.) (2004). *The feminist standpoint theory reader: Intellectual and political controversies*. Psychology Press.

Henry, A. (2005). Chapter four: Black feminist pedagogy: Critiques and contributions. *Counterpoints*, *237*, 89–105.

Hountondji, P. J. (1996). *African philosophy: Myth and reality*. Indiana University Press.

Icaza Garza, R. A. (2018). Social struggles and the coloniality of gender. In R. Shilliam & O. Rutazibwa (Eds.), *Routledge handbook of postcolonial politics* (pp. 58–71). Routledge. doi:10.4324/9781315671192

Icaza Garza, R. A., & Vázquez, R. (2017). Intersectionality and diversity in higher education. *Tijdschrift voor Orthopedagogiek*, *7*(8), 349–357. http://hdl.handle.net/1765/103271

Icaza Garza, R. A., & Vázquez, R. (2018). Diversity or decolonization? Researching diversity at the University of Amsterdam. In *Decolonizing the university*. http://hdl.handle.net/1765/113362.

Jacobs, S. (2013). *Gender and agrarian reforms*. Routledge.

Kane, N. (2007). Frantz Fanon's theory of racialization: Implications for globalization. *Human Architecture: Journal of the Sociology of Self-Knowledge*, *5*(3), 32.

Khader, S. J. (2018). *Decolonizing universalism: A transnational feminist ethic*. Studies in Feminist Philosophy. Oxford University Press.

Kolawole, M. M. (2002). Transcending incongruities: Rethinking feminism and the dynamics of identity in Africa. *Agenda*, *17*(54), 92–98.

82 Beatrice Akala

Lazreg, M. (2005). Decolonizing feminism. In *African gender studies a reader* (pp. 67–80). Palgrave Macmillan.

Lindsey, L. L., & Christie, S. (1997). *Gender roles: A sociological perspective*. Prentice Hall.

Lovet, T., & Smith, D. (1995). *The origins and nature of curriculum. Curriculum: Action on reflection revisited* (3rd ed.). Social Science Press.

MacKinnon, C. A. (1993). Crimes of war, crimes of peace. *UCLA Women's Law Journal, 4*, 59.

Mama, A. (2006). Pursuing gender equality in the African university. *International Journal of African Renaissance Studies, 1*(1), 53–79.

Mama, A. (2011). The challenges of feminism: Gender, ethics, and responsible academic freedom in African Universities. *Journal of Higher Education in Africa/Revue de l'enseignement supérieur en Afrique, 9*(1–2), 1–23.

Mamdani, M. (2008). Higher education, the state, and the marketplace. *Journal of Higher Education in Africa, 6*(1), 1–10.

Manion, C., & Shah, P. (2019). Decolonizing gender and education research: Unsettling and recasting feminist knowledges, power, and research practices. *Gender and Education, 31*(4), 445–451.

Martin, J. (2008). Beyond suffrage: Feminism, education, and the politics of class in the inter-war years. *British Journal of Sociology of Education, 29*(4), 411–423.

Mazrui, A. A. (1978). Superpower ethics: A third world perspective. *Ethics & International Affairs, 1*, 9–21.

Mbembe, A. (2017). Africa in theory. In B. Goldstone & J. Obarrio (Eds.), *African futures: Essays on crisis, emergence, and possibility* (p. 211). University of Chicago Press.

McLaren, M. A. (Ed.). (2017). *Decolonizing feminism: Transnational feminism and globalization*. Rowman & Littlefield.

Mignolo, W. (2003). *The darker side of the renaissance: Literacy, territoriality, and colonization*. University of Michigan Press.

Mignolo, W. D. (2000). *Local histories/global designs: Coloniality, subaltern knowledges, and border thinking*. Princeton University Press.

Mirza, H. S. (2014). Decolonizing higher education: Black feminism and the intersectionality of race and gender. *Journal of Feminist Scholarship, 7*(7), 1–12.

Mohanty, C. (1988). Under Western eyes: Feminist scholarship and colonial discourses. *Feminist Review, 30*(1), 61–88.

Mohanty, C. T. (1989). On race and voice: Challenges for liberal education in the 1990s. *Cultural Critique* (14), 179–208.

Mohanty, C. T. (1998). Crafting feminist genealogies: On the geography and politics of home, nation, and community. In *Talking visions: Multicultural feminism in a transnational age* (pp. 485–500).

Mohanty, C. T. (2003a). "Under western eyes" revisited: Feminist solidarity through anticapitalist struggles. *Signs: Journal of Women in Culture and Society, 28*(2), 499–535.

Mohanty, C. T. (2003b). *Feminism without borders: Decolonizing theory, practicing solidarity*. Duke University Press.

Morley, L. (2006, November). Hidden transcripts: The micropolitics of gender in Commonwealth universities. *Women's Studies International Forum, 29*(6), 543–551.

Mugo, J. K., Nderitu, J. K., & Ruto, S. J. (2015). The 2015 promise of Education for All in Kenya: Missed target or new start? *ZEP: Zeitschrift für internationale Bildungsforschung und Entwicklungspädagogik, 38*(2), 16–21.

Nadar, S. (2014). "Stories are data with soul"–Lessons from black feminist epistemology. *Agenda, 28*(1), 18–28.

Ndlovu-Gatsheni, S. J. (2016). Decolonizing the university and the problematic grammars of change in South Africa. *[Keynote address] Fifth Annual Students Conference on Decolonizing the Humanities and Social Sciences in South Africa/Africa.* University of KwaZulu-Natal (pp. 6–7).

Nix, S., & Perez-Felkner, L. (2019). Difficulty orientations, gender, and race/ethnicity: An intersectional analysis of pathways to STEM degrees. *Social Sciences, 8*(2), 43.

Nussbaum, M. C. (1999). *Sex and social justice*. Oxford University Press.

Nxumalo, F., & Cedillo, S. (2017). Decolonizing place in early childhood studies: Thinking with indigenous onto-epistemologies and black feminist geographies. *Global Studies of Childhood, 7*(2), 99–112.

Nyamnjoh, F. B. (2019). Decolonizing the university in Africa. *Oxford research encyclopedia of politics.* https://doi.org/10.1093/acrefore/9780190228637.013.717

Onsongo, J. (2009). Affirmative action, gender equity and university admissions—Kenya, Uganda, and Tanzania. *London Review of Education, 7*(1), 71–81.

Oyewumi, O. (2003). Introduction: Feminism, sisterhood, and other foreign relations. In O. Oyewumi (Ed.), *African women & feminism: Reflecting on the politics of sisterhood* (pp. 1–24). Africa World.

Parker, P. S., Smith, S. H., & Dennison, J. (2017). Decolonising the classroom. *Tijdschrift voor Genderstudies, 20*(3), 233–247.

Sabzalian, L. (2018). Curricular standpoints and native feminist theories: Why native feminist theories should matter to curriculum studies. *Curriculum Inquiry, 48*(3), 359–382.

Salo, E. (2001). Talking about feminism in Africa. *Agenda, 16*(50), 58–63.

Schiwy, F. (2007). Decolonization and the question of subjectivity: Gender, race, and binary thinking. *Cultural Studies, 21*(2–3), 271–294.

Sleeter, C. E. (2010). Decolonizing curriculum. *Curriculum Inquiry, 40*(2), 193–204. https://www.tandfonline.com/action/showCitFormats?doi=10.1111/j.1467-873X.2010.00477.x

Sparks, T. (2017). Working-class subjectivity in Margaret Harkness's a city girl. *Victorian Literature and Culture, 45*(3), 615–627.

Usher, P. (1996). Feminist approaches to research. In D. Scott & R. Usher (Eds.), *Understanding educational research* (pp. 120–142). Routledge.

wa Thiong'o, N. (1992). *Decolonising the mind: The politics of language in African literature*. East African Publishers.

Weedon, C. (1987). *Feminist practice and poststructuralist theory*. Basil Blackwell.

Wodak, R. (Ed.). (1997). *Gender and discourse*. SAGE.

Woodhull, W. (1993). *Transfigurations of the Maghreb: Feminism, decolonization, and literatures*. University of Minnesota Press

Yenika-Agbaw, V. (2014). Black Cinderella: Multicultural literature and school curriculum. *Pedagogy, Culture & Society, 22*(2), 233–250.

Young, I. M. (1990). *Throwing like a girl: And other essays in feminist philosophy and social theory*. Indiana University Press.

7 Knowledge Democracy and Feminist Epistemic Struggle in African Universities

Simon Vurayai

Setting the Context

Knowledge is an important resource for the existence of any society. It has been a common belief that individuals and societies have perished due to a lack of knowledge. History has revealed that all the members of society have been fighting for recognition of their knowledge because it is an important tool for survival. Denying a certain group's equality, liberty, participation, deliberation, respect, tolerance, and access in the process of knowledge production, dissemination, and ownership can be equated to epistemic genocide. The society in which we live is heterogeneous and multicultural. It is made up of people from different races, sexes, classes, and ethnic groups, hence one should expect diverse ways of knowing which should be tolerated and accommodated. The very fact that we are different in society proves that our ways of knowing and what we know cannot be the same. We were all born with valid epistemologies that should be respected and tolerated.

This book has raised the concern that we should tolerate diversity based on rurality, disability, race, ethnicity, and gender. I proffer the argument that these forms of diversity are there for a purpose and for the endurance of the society, hence their epistemological contribution should be recognised. This chapter delves into the feminist struggle and the road to knowledge democracy. Due to the complex nature of the society, the debate will incorporate the influence of the other exclusionary factors that tend to militate against the feminist struggle for epistemic democracy such as race, class, ethnicity, and disability. I place this debate in the African university context considering that the African continent is perceived as lagging behind in various spheres of development that the university should interrogate. Of concern is an observation by Mangolothi (2019) that

> although attaining gender equality in wider society is a slow journey, it is more shocking that the same is true for the higher education sector. After all, it is within these hallowed halls that we push the boundaries of what is possible and question the norms. This is where new knowledge is unearthed, where multidisciplinary approaches to complex social

DOI: 10.4324/9781003228233-7

Knowledge Democracy and Feminist Epistemic Struggle   85

problems are applied, and where innovation is encouraged. Yet here too, the statistics on gender equality paint a dismal picture.

(para. 1)

I also attest that Higher Education (HE) is a frontier for knowledge democracy, yet it is doing less to expedite the process. There is yet a plethora of areas that needs to be addressed because of the complex nature of the intersectionality of the forces that impede knowledge democracy and justice for women in an African university. In a closely related observation in a recent study in South Africa, Akala (2018) notes that

higher education is still grappling with gender inequity and disparities. Blaming the conundrum on appropriating less attention to gender equity vis-à-vis race and social class equities is not far-fetched ... although the policy promotes inclusivity; black women still face more nuanced alienations in terms of social class, race, epistemological access, language, and sexual abuse and harassment.

(p. 228)

Most African countries are putting more effort into access alone and less into other factors that may be important to support women in HE. Access to HE is just an element of democracy and justice that should be granted along with others. Akala (2018) testifies that

we should not take for granted phrases such as "equal opportunities" and "equal access" in policies. Instead, we should seek their meaning and achievement inter alia in earnest for the targeted group. Therefore, gender and gendering are complex and very fragmented. For this reason, formulating transformation interventions on the premise of equality for all does not necessarily guarantee gender equality or gender equity. With this in mind, a "one-size fits all" approach to redressing gender equality is implausible and does not suffice in addressing salient gender injustices.

(p. 226)

I give credence to the argument that, besides access to HE, there is more to what happens in the system that needs to be addressed to ensure that women realise their potential. It may be naïve to assume that access to HE alone translates to knowledge democracy and justice.

This chapter uses desktop research that utilises the most recent secondary data. I, however, refer to the past strategic literature to shed light on the challenges and successes of the struggle to unyoke the trapped feminist voices. I start by presenting a section on the conceptualisation of the critical feminist epistemology which gives me a better background from which to discuss the theoretical framework. I then present the argument that gender is socially created and should not be taken as a natural barrier to knowledge democracy. A detailed account of the state and stock of feminist epistemic justice in

86   *Simon Vurayai*

HE in Africa will follow. Finally, I provide a motivational voice to the struggle before presenting the summary and conclusion.

Conceptualising the Feminist Epistemology

Knowledge is relative, ideological, and subjective to the point that the different versions of the feminist epistemology have a different approach to the same goal of achieving knowledge democracy. For long, women have been relegated and marginalised, hence I argue that there is a need to allow them uninterrupted participation in the epistemic space. They have the right to question some bad practices, myths, and dogmas that have been prevailing with detrimental effects on the efficacy of women in epistemology. According to Anderson (2020), feminist epistemologies take seriously how knowers are enmeshed in social relations that are generally hierarchical while also being historically and culturally specific. Anderson (2020) elaborates that

- Feminist epistemology and the philosophy of science study how gender does and ought to influence our conceptions of knowledge, knowers, and practices of inquiry and justification.
- They identify how dominant conceptions and practices of knowledge attribution, acquisition, and justification disadvantage women and other subordinated groups, and strive to reform them to serve the interests of these groups.
- Feminist epistemologists trace these failures to flawed conceptions of knowledge, knowers, objectivity, and scientific methodology. They offer diverse accounts of how to overcome these failures. They also aim to (1) explain why the entry of women and feminist scholars into different academic disciplines has generated new questions, theories, methods, and findings; (2) show how gender and feminist values and perspectives have played a causal role in these transformations; (3) promote theories that aid egalitarian and liberation movements; and (4) defend these developments as epistemic advances.

In a more recent study, Chitsamatanga et al. (2018) traced the history of the feminist epistemic struggle in Zimbabwe and attest that women still lag behind in their participation in epistemic issues, particularly in production and dissemination of knowledge. Men monopolise the ownership of knowledge in institutions of learning. They observe that, "Academic publishing is suffering at the hands of hegemonic inequalities that privilege preconceived ideals of masculinity and maleness over femininity and femaleness, thus hindering the career trajectory of females" (Chitsamatanga et al., 2018, p. 77). I endorse that there is a need to interrogate diverse factors that militate against the full participation of women in the epistemic sphere because they affect the production and dissemination of knowledge.

Knowledge Democracy and Feminist Epistemic Struggle   87

Theoretical Framework

In their struggle against patriarchy, feminist movements have developed in many versions, for example, radical, liberal, Marxist, socialist. Budig and Jones (2008) acknowledge that feminist theories are varied and diverse. All analyse women's experiences of gender subordination, the roots of women's oppression, how gender inequality is perpetuated, and offer differing remedies for gender inequality. Jackson (1998, p. 12) avers that,

> feminist social theory has been concerned with understanding fundamental inequalities between women and men and with analyses of male power over women. Its basic premise is that male dominance derives from the social, economic, and political arrangements specific to particular societies.

This chapter rests on the critical feminist theory of knowledge.

I chose the critical feminist theory because it refines the traditional versions of feminism that focus primarily on gender disparities whilst ignoring the intersectionality of complex factors embedded in the process of hegemony and oppression of women. Martin (2003) elaborates that critical feminist theory focusses on the intersections of gender with, for example, race, ethnicity, and class. The history of colonialism and exploitation of Africa suggests that more challenges were added to gender to compound the disparities that African women face. Akala and Divala (2016) recently acknowledged that Black women suffered triple marginalisation: race, social class, and sexism.

In a study in South Africa, Naicker (2013, para 2) notes that,

> racial and gender grouping under the policy of apartheid profoundly shaped the South African society and resulted in rampant inequalities. While women suffered more than black men, exploitation and discrimination were gross for both groups. Empirical research has revealed disturbing subtexts of racism, classism, and sexism within the academy and the endemic structures that marginalised women and black men.

I acknowledge that some corrective steps have been taken to reduce gender disparities in Africa. However, I maintain that the pace to knowledge democracy and epistemic justice for women still leaves a lot to be desired. For example Ramohai (2019), in a recent study, admits that the racial, gender and class divisions that characterised apartheid South Africa presented insurmountable challenges to the higher education contexts. While all higher education institutions in South Africa are working hard to transform, Black women still face numerous challenges on upward mobility, research success, and overcoming gender-based epistemological stereotypes (Ramohai, 2019).

According to de Saxe (2006), the critical feminist theory calls on us to reconsider our existing understandings of knowledge, power, and spaces of empowerment. It is important to have an understanding of the basic tenets of critical feminist theory in order to fully make an application when

88 *Simon Vurayai*

interrogating knowledge democracy and epistemic justice. According to Geisinger (2011), critical feminism is built on the following premises:

- Gender oppression is endemic in our society. It is normal, ordinary, and ingrained into society, making it often difficult to recognise.
- Traditional claims of gender neutrality and objectivity must be contested to reveal the self-interests of the dominant (male) groups.
- Social justice platforms and practices are the only way to eliminate gender discrimination and other forms of oppression and injustice.
- The experiential knowledge of women or their "unique voice" is valid, legitimate, and critical for understanding the persistence of gender inequality, and these unique voices are often demonstrated through storytelling and counter-narratives.
- Women are differentially discriminated against depending on the interests of the dominant group and depending upon the intersections of their identities.
- History and historical contexts must be taken into consideration to challenge policies and practices that affect women.
- Critical feminist theory must be interdisciplinary.

(pp. 10–11)

Adopting the critical feminist theory calls for women to keep on questioning and contesting the endemic gender oppression which is often concealed. The so-called equality policies in HE need to be evaluated concerning the history of epistemic struggle and the current status of women. There is a need to weave interdisciplinary approaches to understand the complex nature of the impediments that women face due to intersecting factors to thoroughly eliminate the oppression, inequalities, and injustices.

The interdisciplinary and multidisciplinary nature of the critical feminist theory gives it a repertoire of roles that guide the route to knowledge democracy in HE and related spheres. This helps to capture all elusive forms of injustices. De Saxe (2006) maintains that critical feminism plays the following roles:

- It offers alternative ways of looking at emancipating oneself from the institutionalisation of oppression.
- It is always evolving and transforming in ways that consistently develop new methodologies of resistance.
- It offers new ways to question the hegemonic nature of institutions as well as to listen and learn about the many diverse sources of empowerment.
- It creates spaces to begin and renew vital conversations. This conversation will, no doubt, be the starting point for revolutionary and transformative change.
- It enables us to question and resituate our current definition and understanding of true emancipatory and equitable education for all.
- It takes the diverse methods and forms of resistance as means to think differently about social justice.

(pp. 198–200)

Knowledge Democracy and Feminist Epistemic Struggle   89

Institutions of learning indeed need to be interrogated. It should not be taken for granted that all has been well from the time more women were granted more access. The critical feminist lenses see beyond access as they try to interrogate issues of participation and empowerment among other transformative processes that facilitate epistemic justice.

Knowledge Democracy and the Feminist Epistemic Struggle

The road to knowledge democracy from the feminist account has been rough and thorny. I proffer the argument that to attain democracy and justice, the African university needs various processes and transformations. It is not an event. I, therefore, give a brief account of the course of the feminist epistemic struggle to the present situation. Jackson and Jones (1998) acknowledge that

> feminist theory has been seeking to analyse the conditions which shape women's lives and to explore cultural understandings of what it means to be a woman. It was initially guided by the political aims of the Women's Movement—the need to understand women's subordination and our exclusion from, or marginalisation within, a variety of cultural and social arenas.
>
> (p. v)

I endorse the idea that critical feminist theory has contributed to important strides and concerted efforts in improving the position of women in HE in Africa. As African countries were gaining independence from colonial rule, there were numerous attempts to correct colonial disparities. One such corrective work was the massification of education. The massification of HE systems has been associated with increasing access for those who have been absent or excluded traditionally. In most contexts, this has been realised by increasing female participation, alongside increasing access for minority groups, the disabled, mature and non-residential students (Dunne & Sayed, 2002, p. 53). Female enrolment increased in HE and this has just been a stepping stone in the knowledge democracy and epistemic struggle.

I contend that there is still a plethora of inequalities even though enrolment for women in HE has increased. Various inequalities need to be addressed. Dunne and Sayed (2002) have noted the existence of the following disparities:

- Increased female access has not been associated with widened access.
- Female academics are unable to take up opportunities for decision-making offered through decentralisation.
- There is a great need for female staff representation as an indicator of more responsive and equitable HE institutions.
- Increased female student enrolments have not been matched by corresponding increases in female staff appointments or retention.
- The subject stereotype shows the predictable minimal proportions of females in the science-based subjects.

90 *Simon Vurayai*

In a related study in Zimbabwe, Njaya (2015) note the following common challenges that women in HE need to address to realise fair emancipation, knowledge democracy, and justice.

- Household commitments and responsibilities.
- Lack of financial resources and poverty.
- Illiteracy and lack of formal primary and secondary education.
- Lack of empowerment.
- Cultural and religious restrictions that prohibit the girl child from going to school.
- Low self-esteem, that is, women have an inferiority complex.
- Preference of male children over female.
- More educated (and financially-independent) women threaten men's dominant status.
- Fears and misconceptions that educated women do not conform to African traditions.
- Lack of appreciation of the value of university education.
- Early marriages and social inhibitions against women pursuing education after marriage.
- Married women "live" in the comfort of their husbands' income and do not see the value of university education.
- Some husbands are jealous of women's advancement and thus deny their wives university education.
- A societal perception that the sole occupation of a woman is to bear children, look after the husband and children, and undertake domestic work.

(p. 86)

I argue that the presence of such disparities implies that there is still more to do in the struggle to knowledge democracy and justice in HE. Women have a mammoth task at hand. The following section gives a detailed account of the state of affairs in selected African countries which I infer represent the rest.

Higher Education and the State of Feminist Epistemic Justice in Africa

The history of the feminist struggle to epistemic democracy suggests that there are many sites on which the battle has been fought, that is, family, religion, economy, legal system, science and technology, mass media, and others. I will make reference to such sites, but the centre and primary focus in this chapter is the African university. According to Dunne and Sayed (2002),

> as many African countries achieved independence in the 1960s, Higher Education institutions were established as symbols of the newly found nationhood and as the new engines for autonomous and autarchic development. The founding of these institutions symbolised the independence and unity of nation-states after often protracted struggles against

divise colonial rule. Ironically, however, these universities were characterised by the transplantation of European models of education.

(p. 53)

I confirm that gender and gendering in HE are very complex. I am going to interrogate issues relating to access, equality, empowerment, participation, and autonomy in knowledge democracy and justice. Creating an enabling environment for women academics, particularly Black women in African institutions of higher education, is still an enormous challenge. The work also demonstrates the pervasive presence of unequal and discriminatory practices in higher education and the need for a truly inclusive and equitable working environment (Naicker, 2013). I evince that there have been tremendous attempts to work on access to HE. However, I show that some fields of knowledge have long been inaccessible to women. I also attempt to place my argument in the historical context to expose the multiple factors that hinder knowledge democracy and justice for women.

Gender and the Curriculum in HE

Knowledge has been used as a divisive tool to acquire power, status, and prestige in HE in Africa.

The curriculum in HE symbolically used femininity and masculinity in preparing girls and boys for their gender roles while excluding them from participating meaningfully in prominent societal activities such as denying women adequate participation in politics, decision-making processes, the economy, and nation-building.

(Akala, 2018, p. 236)

As such, boys and girls, men and women were and are still channelled into different fields of knowledge with different rewards. According to Dunne and Sayed (2002),

A look at the other end of the subject stereotype shows the predictable minimal proportions of females in the science-based subjects. Natural Sciences, Maths and Computing, and Engineering consistently have female cohorts well below their national HE average. These subjects claim the lowest proportions of female students, with the Natural Sciences claiming larger proportions of female students than Maths and Computing and Engineering together.

(p. 60)

Akala (2018, p. 228) agrees that in South Africa,

abstractions from emerging literature indicate that very few women are pursuing Science, Technology, Engineering, and Mathematics (STEM)

92   *Simon Vurayai*

science-related courses. Data indicates that most women are concentrated in humanities, social sciences, education, economics, and management sciences as well as the arts. Similar data shows that very few women enrol in engineering, built environment, and science-related courses. Nationally, data from 2007 demonstrate that men dominate engineering, science, and technology (57%), women dominate other fields: business, commerce and management (56%), education (73%), and human and social science (59%).

A similar trend was noted in Botswana where, for example, in 2002 just over one-quarter of the cohort in Maths and Computing were female, but this was less than one percent of the female students (Dunne & Sayed, 2002, p. 61). This suggests that altogether very few students take this subject at HE level in the country. Both Maths and Computing and Engineering remain consistently unattractive to female students across all these Sub-Saharan African countries (Dunne & Sayed, 2002). In Zimbabwe, a study by Njaya (2015) in one university concurs that underrepresentation of women was more pronounced in the three faculties of Commerce and Law, Arts and Education and Science and Technology, but the pattern was completely reversed for the Faculty of Applied Social Sciences.

In this faculty, the enrolment of female students surpassed that of males. In the Faculty of Science and Technology, women were underrepresented in science and mathematics courses. Although science by its nature is difficult and challenging, compared to their male counterparts, this places women at a disadvantage.

(Njaya, 2015, p. 86)

It will be myopic to look at the underrepresentation of women, particularly in STEM subjects in HE. Having critical feminist lenses helps us to see beyond the present situation. It is important to consider what is happening in secondary and primary schools. According to Dunne and Sayed,

too few students in Sub-Saharan Africa complete secondary with mathematics and science. Thus, the problem of female access and inclusion is related to the question of supply from the school sector. If girls are not being prepared for mathematics and science in the secondary school sector, then higher education institutions will find it difficult to increase enrolment of both students and staff in these areas. Nonetheless, higher education institutions, as is the case in some South African institutions, can play a more proactive role in dealing with this problem.

(2002, p. 63)

I attest that the problem of underrepresentation of female students in HE has its roots in primary and secondary education and even beyond. It is these spheres that need to be interrogated and transformed as well to have fair

Knowledge Democracy and Feminist Epistemic Struggle   93

access of women to STEM subjects. Beyond HE, we still see the persistence of this underrepresentation of women. For example, by 2017 in South Africa, of the 211 academics who were considered active scientists in the country, 78% were White, and only 17% were Black women (Ramohai, 2019).

Gender and Research in HE

It would be naïve to say that all women in Africa face the same predicaments related to democracy and injustices in HE. Besides, the underrepresentation of women in HE also translates to similar or reduced proportions in participation in research activities and research outputs. A study by Tyatya (2020) which revealed a dearth in the participation of Black females at the doctoral level, translates to the post-doctoral and even professorship levels in South Africa. In 2019, females comprised only 34% of the National Research Foundation (NRF) rated researchers, with White females being the dominant racial group within the female rated researchers' category (Tyatya, 2020). According to Ramohai (2019), Black women from urban areas and advantaged schooling backgrounds have a much greater opportunity to obtain employment in higher education; women from rural areas and disadvantaged schooling backgrounds may find themselves marginalised by socio-economic systems when they search for employment.

> In 2017, white academics made up 47% of instructional and research staff despite making up less than 8% of the total population. The percentage share of white academics is particularly high in former white-only institutions such as Stellenbosch University, University of Pretoria and Rhodes University (where white academics comprised 77%, 76% and 70%, respectively) with the opposite being true for former black-only universities. When we look at gender, white female academics account for approximately the same percentage (25.3%) of instructional and research staff as African, coloured and Indian female academics combined.
>
> (Tyatya, 2020)

The research activities and related participation by women also determine how they excel in HE compared to their counterparts. It is important to note that gaining access to HE and excelling rates for women are important indicators of epistemic justice. A related study reveals that,

> According to statistics published by the Council for Higher Education, in South Africa, there were 56527 academic staff in 2017. Of these, 13531 held PhDs, of which only 42.06% were held by women academics. The council also found that of the 3040 senior managers in the higher education sector, only 44.76% were women. Women academics made up only 29% of professors, 41% of associate professors and 46% of senior lecturers.
>
> (Mangolothi, 2019, para 2)

94 *Simon Vurayai*

I proffer the vindication that compromised access to, and participation in, knowledge production and ownership by women in HE is also mirrored in the ratios of how they progress and excel within the system. One would rarely expect a different matrix table when it comes to Black women PhD holders and professors.

The active participation of academics in HE can be noted by their research publications. There is overwhelming evidence that women academics in most African countries still lag behind their male counterparts in this regard. Other researchers have attributed low research output by African women to poor funding. Some countries have tried to address this disparity, but the evidence is overwhelming that more needs to be done. In South Africa, Shober (2014) noted that,

> despite opportunities and other funding resources such as the National Research Foundation Thuthuka program which provides research monies for women and the previously disadvantaged, some female academics still feel restricted in voicing their concerns about the barriers they encounter in higher education.
>
> (p. 319)

In Zimbabwe, Chitsamatanga et al. (2018) lament that the high rejection rate of research manuscripts is also one of the reasons why female academics fail to publish and are unable to develop their careers.

> For instance, in one university in Zimbabwe, male academics contributed 83 percent of research output and articles produced. If comparisons were to be made, the picture in South Africa is not at all different from the Zimbabwean situation. On an international sphere, studies indicate that male academics publish 8 percent more articles.
>
> (Chitsamatanga et al., 2018, p. 78)

Limited exposure to and involvement in research activities by women can also be attributed to a lack of mentoring and the patriarchal politics of journals. In a study by Naicker (2013) in South Africa, a key finding was that many senior scholars were reluctant to offer junior rank academics support, particularly women.

Another challenge was the dissemination of scholarly material in journals. It emerged that most mainstream journals are controlled by what one participant called an "old boy's network" and, as such, are not receptive to the kind of work that women academics are engaged in, that is, research that is community based and written from a non-Western perspective or research that is written from the perspective of gender. One participant noted that she would not submit her research to a gender-focussed journal because her senior colleagues viewed such a journal as being weak (Naicker, 2013).

I attest that the lack of mentoring in research can have debilitating effects, such as high rejection of research by women scholars. If men erect barriers to

Knowledge Democracy and Feminist Epistemic Struggle 95

publication in which they discount or write out the contributions by women in their patriarchally networked journals, I envisage the scholarship efforts by women being paralysed.

Gender and Positions of Power in HE

The terms for promotion in HE are directly linked to research and the qualification one possesses. Underrepresentation of women in the same would mean a stumbling block to their chances to rise to higher echelons of decision-making. I agree that power and knowledge are intertwined. The absence of women in the rungs of authority, power, and decision-making in HE undoubtedly offers them no or fewer opportunities to realise knowledge democracy and justice. According to Chitsamatanga et al. (2018 p. 77), "the dearth of published work by female academics impacts negatively on getting better salaries, advancement and most importantly, job security". In Zimbabwe, "concerns about women under-representation in positions of decision making, strategic planning, organizational development and their performance within distance education institutions has been the major focus of debates in higher education" (Shava & Ndebele, 2014, p. 359). There are also similar concerns in South Africa, Kenya, and the rest of the African countries.

I testify that few women in HE are participating in leadership and decision-making positions in African universities. This is likely to affect the participation of women in knowledge production and ownership. According to Tyatya (2020), transformation cannot only be viewed from an access lens; transformation goes beyond just access—it encompasses the progression of Black and female academics to senior academic rank and leadership of universities. In a study in South Africa, it was noted that at the lecturer and junior lecturer level, women dominated in numbers. This shows that although women make up the majority of the workforce, their representation at decision-making levels remains low (Mangolothi, 2019). In Zimbabwe, a similar pattern has been noted:

> The fact that men were assigned a monopoly of access to higher managerial positions of authority and power in organizations and the public sphere, with women restricted ..., has come under attack in both developed and most developing countries. While efforts seem to be in place to accelerate the advancement of women, the number of women who achieve senior management positions is still disproportionate to the number of women employed in the universities.
>
> (Shava & Ndebele, 2014, p. 359)

Most recent studies in Zimbabwe and South Africa reveal that women are still excluded from managerial positions in HE. The positions such as director, dean, pro-vice-chancellor, and vice-chancellor are still a preserve for men. In a study carried out in South Africa it was found that the higher education sector is still dominated by white men, many of whom occupy management positions. Out of 26 higher education institutions, only four are led by women—Thoko Mayekiso at the University of Mpumalanga, Sibongile Muthwa at Nelson Mandela University, Mamokgethi Phakeng at the University of Cape Town, and Xoliswa Mtose at the University of Zululand.

(Mangolothi, 2019, para 2)

A more recent study confirms the earlier matrix of power in decision-making positions in HE in South Africa.

There has been a gradual change in the race profile of vice-chancellors (VCs) at some historically White institutions such as the universities of Cape Town, Witwatersrand, Pretoria, and Johannesburg, but only one of these VCs is female. We need to give Black females who have excelled in their fields of research leadership opportunities, but even more importantly, we need to build the cadre of Black female academics so that the pool is much wider for females to take over leadership positions in academia (Tyatya, 2020).

There is an attempt by researchers to raise other reasons why few women occupy the positions of power and critical decision-making in HE. Some factors that have been raised are hostility from men, stereotypes, family-role conflict, intraconflict, and lack of mentoring support. I can attest that all these factors compound to militate against women in knowledge democracy and epistemic justice. "Interestingly, myths, stereotypes, and prejudices related to the abilities and attitudes of women are seen to be among obstacles encountered for the representation of women in management positions" (Chabaya et al., 2009, p. 240). Shava and Ndebele (2014, p. 366) add that:

> It is also argued that women's participation in positions of authority is seen to be difficult, usually thwarted by men who discourage their participation in these positions and see their activism as deviant. This 'glass ceiling' which is a metaphor for the invisible barrier that prevents women from advancing in their organizations to senior leadership positions is created by invisible forces of culture, habit, and power.

By using critical feminist lenses, one gets a clear picture of the mammoth forces that militate against the empowerment of women towards knowledge democracy and justice. Mangolothi (2019, para 4) opines that

> With few women at the top management level, institutions remain patriarchal environments in which the particular difficulties that women face, and their specific needs, are ignored. Career progression for women is further delayed by other factors such as enabling cultures geared towards the advancement of men, societal perceptions that men are better leaders, and the low number of women who apply for senior and top management positions because of a workplace culture that prides itself on long,

Knowledge Democracy and Feminist Epistemic Struggle 97

intensive workdays that may affect a woman's other responsibilities. Besides, women at senior and top management levels often have to deal with hostility from men—and they do the same work as men but earn less.

From the anecdotes above, I endorse that women are subjected to hostility in their attempt to occupy positions of authority. They face resistance from men who try to justify their power in a subtle and concealed manner. A hostile environment is fragmented and hard to manage. The management positions will become difficult for women who have other extra family and societal roles that are demanded by the patriarchal society.

I also assert that women lack support to rise to positions of authority in HE because of hostility from their male counterparts. There is also a challenge of intraconflict (Mangolothi, 2019; Shava & Ndebele, 2014). Some women also "pull" them down when they are trying to progress. I note that the hostility from fellow women can be very incapacitating.

The intraconflict dynamics between women is a neglected discussion. Many women are reluctant to support other women once they have been appointed to leadership positions. Others take on the same behaviours as their male counterparts, leading to them being seen as too masculine in their leadership style and penalised for it, or keeping other women from climbing the ladder (Mangolothi, 2019).

An earlier related study also expressed concern about the rate of intraconflict:

> The moment a woman occupied a senior position, she encountered problems such as loneliness, isolation, lack of acceptance, particularly as a result of rejection by peers and subordinates of both genders. One of the woman directors at the national centre noted that the first time a woman received criticism or the first time she failed, she would code it as a sign that she was inferior and that she should never have tried to become a manager in the first place.
>
> (Shava & Ndebele, 2014, p. 366)

I opine that intraconflict can be more devastating and self-defeating in the struggle for feminist epistemic democracy and justice. Men can also use it as an excuse and opportunity to weaken the feminist front in the struggle.

Besides institutional conflict, research suggests that women fail to rise in HE due to the lack of spousal support. They are compelled to work close to where they can attend to other family obligations and responsibilities, thereby limiting their opportunities. Chitsamatanga et al. (2018, p. 85) opine that

> family and spousal support are crucial especially in terms of emotional support. The reason being, lack of advancement of female academics is tied to the disproportionate burden of family responsibilities, lack of family support, deeply entrenched cultural beliefs, and work-life balance.

98 *Simon Vurayai*

An earlier study by Chabaya et al. (2009) confirms that women were found not to be prepared to take up positions away from their husbands and children. "Given a choice between career advancement in places away from the family and staying with one's family, most women appeared to prefer the latter" (Chabaya et al., 2009, p. 239).

As discussed above, there is a plethora of hurdles that women face in their struggle to knowledge democracy and justice which cannot be exhausted in this chapter. I am convinced that by using the critical feminist lenses, more challenges can be exposed and strategies devised. I agree that women have a valid right to define, control, disseminate, and own knowledge in society and HE, just like any other resource in society. In the next section, I present some of the strategies to empower women to continue with the struggle.

Defining the Pathways to Women's Empowerment

The road to democracy and justice in all facets of life is not an easy one. It is a process, not an event. There is a need to utilise every atom of the effort that has been contributed by others as presented in history and take the struggle to the ultimate unyoking of the trapped African feminist voices. I argue that women and men need to revisit the social institutions which are sites of hostility and barriers to epistemic democracy and justice. I proffer the suggestions that stem from the challenges in access to some fields of knowledge, research output, conflict dynamics, power, and promotion in HE. I believe that it is important for men and those in privileged positions to acknowledge that access only does not translate to democracy and justice. There is an excess of hurdles that must be addressed.

> There is a need within the academy to build social cohesion. We cannot uphold the denialism that inequalities do not exist. These inequalities are often dismissed as baseless accusations of overreaction. Moreover, inequalities and discrimination often remain unnoticed, especially when those who do not experience them fail to understand how deeply offensive/wounding they are. We must also admit that those who find themselves on the fringes of employment at academic institutions are more likely to encounter discrimination. Social cohesion within the academy means that all individuals are made to feel secure in their jobs and an acknowledgment and recognition of their unique contribution.
>
> (Naicker, 2013, para 8)

It is necessary to reconsider the plight of women beyond the call for access in HE. I agree that more strategies need to be devised and implemented to tackle the complexity of the feminist hurdles to epistemic justice. In Zimbabwe, Njaya (2015) has noted the role that has been played by distance education in empowering women, particularly on the element of access.

Knowledge Democracy and Feminist Epistemic Struggle   99

> Open and distance learning helped women to circumvent constraints of time, space, resources, and socio-economic barriers thereby significantly contributing to their empowerment. A majority of women took a break to attend to their multiple duties either during or after undergraduate studies.
>
> (Njaya, 2015, p. 83)

Due to its flexibility and mode of delivery, the above barriers of access to higher education make distance education the ultimate choice for women (Njaya, 2015). It was in recognition of the challenges that limit access to tertiary education and the inability of conventional universities to admit more students in an alternative model that the government established Zimbabwe Open University (ZOU) as a key measure to widen access to higher education. (Njaya, 2015). I agree that, among other strategies, the introduction of distance education has been a corrective strategy to affirm access for women to HE. This strategy has worked in Zimbabwe to address the role conflict that women faced, while at the same time progressing in academic and professional studies. They could still study and attend to family responsibilities and obligations. To a certain extent, this model has worked in favour of women whose spouses would not allow them to further their education away from the family, in the case of most conventional models in HE.

In addressing the problem of access to certain fields of knowledge in HE, affirmative action policies have been adopted in Africa. Some universities have decided to lower the entry qualification of female students in some fields. I agree that if used genuinely without denigrating women, it could be an avenue to knowledge democracy and justice. However, Mareva (2014, p. 175) maintains that

> affirmative action should be implemented with moderation so that male students do not feel overly disadvantaged and at the same time females do not feel belittled … in general and teachers, in particular, should stop perpetuating prejudices and stereotypes against the girl child.

Affirmative action can also be done by opening more funding opportunities for women in HE and research activities. In Zimbabwe Chitsamatanga et al. (2018, p. 87) recommend that

> there should be formalised mentoring to assist female academics to realise career development within the academia under the tutelage of senior academics regardless of gender. This may be achieved by encouraging female academics to attain PhDs and also offering them scholarships to further their studies, research funds and sabbatical leave.

I agree that there have been some gender-responsive programmes and policies in HE in some African countries, but they seem not to translate to action. Despite South Africa having one of the most progressive legal frameworks

100 *Simon Vurayai*

for gender equity in the world, it is sad to note that some universities do not have policies, systems, and programmes in place to ensure gender transformation (Mangolothi, 2019). Most of the polices are cosmetic and idle on paper, hence they lack proper enforcement. Moreso,

> A positive gender-responsive organisational culture and transformational leadership should be cultivated in universities. This is significant in imparting self-belief among female academics so that they can aspire to reach the top echelons of university leadership, as well as realising career growth. There is a need to implement programs that talk to and meet the needs of academics, particularly females.
>
> (Chitsamatanga et al., 2018 p. 87)

The legal frameworks and policies should be monitored and evaluated regularly in the spheres of power and authority. I proffer the idea of even sharing proportionally the positions of power, management, and decision-making between men and women; the idea being that without power it may be difficult to realise epistemic democracy and justice.

Women need to unite and avoid intraconflict in the struggle to knowledge democracy and epistemic justice. Women need to support each other to see real change. They should also make it a norm to network and collaborate with colleagues inside and outside their institutions, nationally and internationally (Mangolothi, 2019). Shava and Ndebele (2014, p. 359) recommend "the holding of open and honest discussion forums on gender and equal rights issues involving both men and women and the development of family-friendly culture in universities". I also suggest more powerful support and mentoring networks for African women. These networks should provide services in research, publication, leadership, conflict management, and other spheres that are meant to empower women in the struggle to knowledge democracy and justice. I suggest networking should start at the community and grassroots level up to the continental level.

Summary and Conclusion

This chapter has interrogated gender as a factor that militates against knowledge democracy and the epistemic struggle of women in African HE. I examined the state of knowledge democracy in HE, bearing in mind that it is a strong institution that preaches about the emancipation of women. Despite HE being regarded as the source of hope for the unyoking of trapped voices for women academics, I found it riddled with injustices. This chapter adopted the critical feminist lenses to confront the barriers that prevent women from enjoying the same epistemic space as their male counterparts. Some of the factors that I examined are related to the issues of access and active participation of women in the curriculum, research, and positions of power. There is overwhelming evidence from research that women still lag behind in these areas.

Knowledge Democracy and Feminist Epistemic Struggle 101

Although there are some corrective works, policies, and strategies that have been put in place to empower women, this chapter suggests that more effort is needed to monitor and enforce them to ensure the total emancipation of women in HE. I proffer recommendations such as affirmative action, support and mentoring networks to mitigate these barriers. I also suggest that there is a need for women to shun intraconflict and support each other if they are to overcome the obstructions to knowledge democracy and justice.

References

Akala, B., & Divala, J. (2016). Gender equity tensions in South Africa's post-apartheid higher education: In defence of differentiation. *South African Journal of Higher Education*, *30*(1). https://doi.org/10.20853/30-1-557

Akala, B. M. (2018). Challenging gender equality in South African transformation policies—a case of the White Paper: A programme for the transformation of higher education. *South African Journal of Higher Education*, *32*(3). doi:10.20853/32-3-1521

Anderson, E. (2020, Spring). Feminist epistemology and philosophy of science. In E. N. Zalta (Ed.), *The Stanford Encyclopedia of Philosophy*. https://plato.stanford.edu/archives/spr2020/entries/feminism-epistemology/

Budig, M., & Jones, K. (2008). Feminist theory. In V. N. Parillo (Ed.), *Encyclopedia of social problems*. SAGE Publications. https://doi.org/10.4135/9781412963930

Chabaya, O., Rembe, S., & Wadesango, N. (2009). The persistence of gender inequality in Zimbabwe: Factors that impede the advancement of women into leadership positions in primary schools. *South African Journal of Education*, *29*(2), 235–251. https://doi.org/10.15700/saje.v29n2a259

Chitsamatanga, B. B., Rembe, S., & Shumba, J. (2018). Mentoring for female academics in the 21st century: A case study of a South African university. *International Journal of Gender and Women's Studies*, *6*(1). doi: 10.15640/ijgws.v6n1a5

de Saxe, J. (2006). Conceptualizing critical feminist theory and emancipatory education. *Journal for Critical Education Policy Studies*, *10*(2). ISSN 1740–2743 http://www.jceps.com/wp-content/uploads/PDFs/10-2-06.pdf

Dunne, M. & Sayed, Y. (2002). Transformation and equity: Women and higher education in sub-Saharan Africa. *Higher Education*, *30*(1), 50–65. http://digitalknowledge.cput.ac.za/bitstream/11189/5188/1/Dunne_Mairead_Sayed_Yusuf_Transformation%20and%20Equity%3A%20Women%20and%20Higher%20Education%20in%20Sub-Saharan%20Africa_pdf

Geisinger, B. N. (2011). *Critical feminist theory, rape, and hooking up*. doi: 10.31274/etd-180810-2292

Jackson, S. (1998). Feminist social theory. In S. Jackson & J. Jones (Eds.), *Contemporary feminist theories* (pp. 12–33). Edinburgh University Press. doi: 10.3366/j.ctvxcrxc7.4

Jackson S. & Jones J. (Eds.). (1998). *Contemporary feminist theories*. Edinburgh University Press. doi: 10.3366/j.ctvxcrxc7.4

Mangolothi, B. (2019, 20 September). Advancing gender equality in academia. *Mail & Guardian*. https://mg.co.za/article/2019-09-20-00-advancing-gender-equality-in-academia/

Mareva, R. (2014). Affirmative action by lowering university entry points for females: Great Zimbabwe University students' views. *Global Journal of Interdisciplinary Social Sciences (G.J.I.S.S)*, *3*(4), 173–178. https://www.longdom.org/articles/affirmative-action-by-lowering-university-entry-points-for-females-great-zimbabwe-university-students-views.pdf

102 *Simon Vurayai*

Martin, J. (2003). Feminist theory and critical theory: Unexplored synergies. In *Studying management critically* (pp. 66–91). SAGE Publications. doi: 0.4135/9781446220030.n4

Naicker, L.(2013). The journey of South African women academics with a particular focus on women academics in theological education. *Studia Historia Ecclesiasticae* [online], *39*(1), 325–336. ISSN 2412-4265

Njaya, T. (2015). Women empowerment through open and distance learning in Zimbabwe. *Journal of Humanities and Social Science (IOSR-JHSS)*, *20*(2), Ver. IV, 83–90. e-ISSN: 2279-0837, p-ISSN: 2279-0845. www.iosrjournals.org

Ramohai, J. (2019). A black woman's perspective on understanding transformation and diversity in South African higher education. *Transformation in Higher Education*, *4*. doi: 10.4102/the.v4i0.58

Shava, G. N., & Ndebele, C. (2014). Challenges and opportunities for women in distance education management positions: Experiences from the Zimbabwe Open University (ZOU).*JournalofSocialSciences,40*(3),359–372.doi:10.1080/09718923.2014.11893331

Shober, D. (2014). Women in higher education in South Africa. *Advances in Gender Research*, *19*, 315–332. doi: 10.1108/s1529-212620140000019014

Tyatya, K. (2020, July 22). Time for black women to lead in higher education. *Maverick Citizen* OP-ED. https://www.dailymaverick.co.za/article/2020-07-22-time-for-black-women-to-lead-in-higher-education

8 Globalisation and Commodification of Knowledge Liberating Women's Academic Achievements from Conventional Global Power Hierarchies

Zvisinei Moyo

Introduction

The commodification and globalisation of knowledge have become significant aspects in new academic debates on the recognition of women in their contribution to the knowledge economy. Yang (2006) asserted that the free market philosophy has penetrated the higher education sphere in most English-speaking countries such as Europe, as well as Latin America, and Southeast Asia. Undeniably, the discourse has also affected the African continent. Yang further explained, "Market relevance is becoming the key orientating criterion for the selection of discourses, their relation to each other, their forms and their research" (Yang, 2006, p. 54). The current discourses of competition and profit are alternatively favoured and are rapidly organising and delivering higher education globally. While Yang (2006) problematised the movement of romanticising privatisation of education to the bureau-professional regime of public welfare, I argue that it has profound implications on women who have been disadvantaged through various forms of social inequalities, especially those rooted in patriarchal ideologies. Hence, efforts in pursuit of gender equity have dominated scholarly discussions for a long time. Nonetheless, although achievements thus far do not outweigh the promises of democracy in Zimbabwe, the commodification of higher education in the globalised knowledge economy can unyoke knowledge that has been previously relegated to the shadows simply because of gender. Women have for a long time remained on the margins, regardless of international statutes, several national laws, and institutional instruments adopted to deal with historical colonial injustices and inequality.

Notably, there has been a trend in investigating the promotion of gender equality in academia; for instance, how a gender responsive organisational culture can be promoted to enhance female leadership (Chitsamatanga et al., 2018a), barriers to female leadership and how women can take an active role in addressing their disadvantaged positions (Zvobgo, 2015), as well as alienation of female academics (Gaidzanwa, 2007). In addition, there have been similar findings on the importance of mentoring as a vital tool for the development of female academics (Chitsamatanga et al., 2018b; Mudhovozi et al.,

DOI: 10.4324/9781003228233-8

2013; Ndebele et al., 2013). Other studies focussed on hurdles in career trajectories, regardless of staff development in Zimbabwe and South Africa, and concluded that capacity-building and more financial resources were needed (Chitsamatanga et al., 2018c) and that there was gender inequality (Guzura & Chigora, 2012). Another study, focussing on the extent of policy implementation in the promotion of women leadership, established that of the 96 management positions at the Midlands State University, women constituted 28% and males 72% (Zvobgo, 2014). Two other studies, one on lecturers' promotion to leadership positions in four universities, confirmed a long-established assumption of male dominance in leadership (Mugweni, 2014) and limited implementation of affirmative action (Chitsamatanga et al., 2020), respectively.

Elsewhere, recent research conducted in South Africa on women in higher education showed a persistence of underrepresentation of women in leadership amid programmes like the National Research Foundation (NRF), sponsored by Thuthuka, which provides women and the previously disadvantaged with financial support. However, women continue to face hindrances such as familial roles, gender-related issues, patriarchal stereotypes (Shober, 2014) and underrepresentation of women in senior leadership positions (Moodly & Toni, 2017; Naicker, 2013). Bezuidenhout and Cillers (2010) also investigated the importance of governmental policies on female academics and the commitment of universities in South Africa to adopting and enhancing gender equity promotional programmes. The study was motivated by the continuous challenges faced by female academics in South African higher learning institutions. Unfortunately, this is exacerbated by the system which promotes male academics and a misleading sense of superiority over female academics, which is well supported and sustained to keep the prevailing system intact. Therefore, female academics' achievements and their role in society are barely acknowledged or recognised (Chitsamatanga, 2014).

Most importantly, the above studies illustrate that implementation of gender equity in both Zimbabwean and South African universities is premised on the requirement to acknowledge the value of having in place a mutual approach in addressing issues associated with the emancipation of females and tapping into gender mainstreaming as a tool for promoting gender equality (Guzura, 2017). Nonetheless, previous studies have not focussed on how the commodification of higher education in a globalised knowledge economy can be used as a platform to liberate knowledge from the formerly marginalised and disadvantaged—in this case, Zimbabwean women. Little is known about how the commodification of higher education in a globalised world is enabling Zimbabwean women to transcend the epistemological global hierarchy of power and how the conventional global governance of education, which has further worsened the status of women, is becoming relevant. Therefore, this present research aimed to understand how the purpose of Zimbabwean women in higher education has changed over time due to globalisation, technological advancement, and commodification. It sought to answer the question: In what ways can it be argued that commodification

Liberating Women's Academic Achievements 105

of higher education in a globalised knowledge economy is unyoking women's contributions?

The purpose of higher education has seen the betterment of humanity in relation to the flourishing of ideas, the common good of humanity, and the support of democracy (Nixon, 2010). As this chapter argues, commodification of higher education does have a significant effect on women's knowledge, formerly subjugated to the global governance of education. Henceforth, this chapter summarises the key theoretical issues, rationale, and strategies associated with the commodification of higher education from existing literature in order to create a baseline of understanding about the subject and to set a platform and justification for launching this specific study. It then discusses the positive effect of commodification of higher education in a globalised knowledge economy on the women of Zimbabwe as a previously excluded group.

The chapter critically analyses Zimbabwean higher education with specific reference to universities, drawing upon a variety of written sources including statistics from the demographic distribution of the population. These sources were read and interpreted from personal experience as a woman having grown up in rural areas who faced several hurdles in acquiring a university education. Issues of social inequalities in the funding of higher education are raised and examined as key illustrations of the highest form of discrimination exacerbated by various trajectories affecting women in higher education. Although I grounded my analysis of gender inequality in Zimbabwe's universities in dominant strands, this chapter is also strongly informed by my engagement in gender activism, in struggles against the marginalisation of women amid marketisation of higher education in Zimbabwe.

Background

In order to grasp the purpose and development within higher education, a background perspective is necessary since many of the core values of higher education were established some years ago. As at 2019, the Zimbabwean nation had a total population of 13 447 286; 6 485 676 (48%) being male and 6 961 610 (52%) being female. Out of the 68% of the rural population, 51% were female and 49% were male (Zimbabwe Education Management Information System (EMIS), 2019). Zimbabwe has two ministries of education: the Ministry of Primary and Secondary Education and the Ministry of Higher and Tertiary Education, Science and Technology Development. Since independence in 1980, the number of schools has increased enormously due to the expansion policies aimed at increasing access to education for all. The Zimbabwe Ministry of Primary and Secondary Education's (MoPSE) (2019) statistical report stated that in 2018 there were 6 288 primary schools and 2 878 secondary schools. The country has also seen a phenomenal increase in higher education institutions—from a single university in 1980 to 24 registered universities comprising 14 public and ten private universities (Garwe & Thondhlana, 2018). University enrolment increased from 57 in a single

106 *Zvisinei Moyo*

university to 91 823 in 2017. The Ministry of Higher and Tertiary Education, Science and Technology Development is the custodian of post-secondary education in Zimbabwe. This chapter is concerned about the 75% of primary school and 70% of secondary school learners in rural areas. These disproportions at lower levels of schooling adversely affect gender equality at higher education levels (Guzura & Chigora, 2012).

As shown above, the majority of the Zimbabwean population reside in the reservoirs of poverty (Coltart, 2008) known as rural areas, where socioeconomic realities put them at a disadvantage. Women dominate this portion of the rural population and their lives are constrained by circumstances of location. These circumstances make it difficult for schools to offer high quality curricula (Mandina, 2012) as compared to urban areas which are economically developed and enjoy relatively greater prosperity. Given that patriarchy is more concentrated in the rural areas where transformation is slowly taking place, the high cost of sending children to university may disadvantage girls more than boys. These factors (being poor and living in remote areas) add another layer to what women are already grappling with (Organisation for Economic Co-operation and Development [OECD], 2011). In addition, the historic economic meltdown of Zimbabwe has triggered one of the worst episodes of poverty—limiting access to higher education. Consequently, in the failing economy, parents may not see any benefits derived from educating their female children who may least consider education as a tool capable of transforming lives.

Despite all available evidence that convincingly emphasises the gains of colonial independence, education bottlenecks in the form of gender inequalities still persist in Zimbabwe and the rest of Africa. The gender gap is universal throughout the continent (Shober, 2014). Among the key policy areas of concern in the gender discourse is education, which is an important tool in fighting poverty and empowering women. Education is a prerequisite tool for the well-being of the population, as it helps people make economic, social, and political decisions.

Higher education is a contested topic that cannot be debated outside the confines of a specific society within which social, political, and economic characteristics interfere with the gender discourse within that society. Teferra (2014) stressed that higher education systems in Africa have not only remained unequal across countries and sub-regions, but massively unequal and largely associated with economic status, gender, and origin (rural/urban). Therefore, the highest income quintile is more likely to access higher education, for example in Malawi, where 91.9% of students in higher education come from the highest income bracket (World Bank, 2010).

The economic and political demise of Zimbabwe has privileged causes and consequences of the crisis, casting shadows on the lamentable marginalisation of the low socio-economic status groups—women and girls. I agree that education is an indispensable dimension in empowering women in Zimbabwe, Africa, and the world over. Undoubtedly, the prevailing context of the capitalist economy, characterised by individualism, makes the quest for gender

Liberating Women's Academic Achievements 107

equity difficult to realise. The introduction of a proto-nationalistic discourse claiming a metanarrative force is backed up by Pan-Africanists and spurned anti-imperialist sentiments throughout Africa and globally. The education system mirrors and is shaped by the political and economic context (Matereke, 2011) marked by policy inconsistencies. Matereke (2011) argued that post-colonial leaders relied on the colonial structures of industrial capitalism to draw material wealth for personal gain while they claimed to dismantle these same structures.

The Concept of Commodification

The concept of commodification originated from Marx's sentiment of commodity fetishism which he viewed as a situation where economic forms of capital obfuscate underlying social relations (Marx, 1952). The process of commodification organises the provision of goods and services in a business form. It is used to describe how consumer culture is ultimately ingrained in daily lives through a variety of barely noticeable processes. Its effects on higher education in Zimbabwe are inescapable. Consequently, there are changes in the production of discourses and the conditions of knowledge, as well as a general transformation in the nature of social relations (Yang, 2006) because of the removal of traditional structures and boundaries which have sustained modern ways of thinking, setting aside moral spheres and obligations in preference for economic ones.

Yang (2006) highlighted that the concept of commodification is closely related to commercialisation, privatisation, corporatisation, and marketisation. These are underpinned by similar views in market ideologies; that is, the language, logic, and principle of private market exchange into public institutions and taking control of corporate culture over every aspect as a result of the rising trend of neoliberal globalisation that has brought significant changes in social affairs over the past three decades. Capital is increasingly taking command of the world order, like never before (McLaren, 2005). The purpose and potential of education is defined by economism. Higher education institutions have become commodity-producing enterprises, best described as capitalisation (Hwami, 2013). They are restructured according to a capitalist accumulation model. This includes bringing in private service providers to deliver public services and reordering existing public sector delivery into ways similar to that of the private sector and that have similar consequences in terms of practices, values, and identities. It can be argued that competitive ranking among universities is a form of commodification and does influence the purpose and values of universities.

Further, Yang (2006) indicated that commodification happens at the administrative, industrial, and instrumental levels; at the administration level in that the higher education institutions run like an enterprise, focussing on budgetary cost-effectiveness, seeking resources, product evaluation and corresponding adjustment, new hiring policies, and new relationships between teachers and students. On the other hand, the instrumental level treats the

108 *Zvisinei Moyo*

entire process of teaching and learning as cost-effect-driven, focussing on learning and teaching as a necessary step for producing a product, readjusting the purposes of learning and teaching, depersonalisation, and utility-oriented curricular objectives. The distinction of a morally responsible university which works for the benefit of the public good and to better the society seems to be in contrast to the more overall commodification of the society, where the values of the university seem to be concerned with competition, ranking lists, and economic gain from the usability of knowledge. This has resulted in the commodification of knowledge serving the instrumental ends of the globalised knowledge economy.

Globalisation

Placket (2012) described globalisation as characterised by the interconnectedness of societies and cultures into a global community. Johnston-Anumonwo and Doane (2011) stressed that there is an increase of global interconnectedness through the velocity of global interactions. These schools of thought show that the world is incorporated into a single global socio-economic unit (Maringe, 2009). To understand the concept of globalisation, Cohen and Kennedy (2007) identified six factors: changing concept of time and space, intensification of cultural interactions and flows, communalism, prominence of transnational organisations, interconnectedness and blurring of boundaries, and synchronisation of all dimensions. The world is now driven by a knowledge economy as opposed to a previously money-based economy (Maringe, 2009). However, globalisation has been criticised as a force facilitating internationalisation in the form of social colonisation. Some perspectives have referred to it as a modern form of spreading values of the West and the United States of America in imperialistic and neocolonialist ways, resulting in the loss of national identity (Maringe, 2009). Moyo and Perumal (2018) have pointed out that no dominant countries lose freedom of choice.

On the positive side, globalisation has seen a rapid increase in international mobility of goods and opportunity driven by technological advancement and market liberalisation of policies. Indeed, it has impacted differently on different countries, communities, families, and individual people (Onyido, 2013). The constant flow of knowledge, ideas, and people has rendered it a possible way to eradicate poverty because of the expansion of the labour market. Innovation and modern qualities promote equality, diversity, and engagement of different cultures (Placket, 2012). The modern ways of communication have shrunk the barriers of time and distance. These are explained within the context of formerly marginalised women in higher education.

Funding and Financing of University Education in Zimbabwe

According to Garwe and Thondhlana (2018), universities are funded through fiscal allocations, student levies, donations, and income generated from the institutions' resource mobilisation initiatives. The authors further noted that

Liberating Women's Academic Achievements   109

the government used to meet 82.4% of university funding, as evidenced in the allocation of the biggest share of the national budget in the period between 1980 and 2000. Since then, funding of higher education has declined and the country has not yet put into practice a scientific funding formula for public higher education institutions such as other African countries like South Africa. Institutions of higher learning rely on indistinct methods and conceivably unjust allocation processes. The private institutions utilise other sources of funds; that is, students' fees and levies pitched at full cost levels paid directly to the institutions' accounts without government interference (Garwe & Thondhlana, 2018). Although access to higher education has increased significantly since 1980, it remains limited to the few who can pay the fees. This is shown by the gross higher education enrolment which has remained at 8% regardless of the recorded literacy levels, in comparison to South Africa with 18%.

Against the backdrop of unclear funding systems, the Zimbabwean government introduced the pay as you earn paying policies, causing indescribable pain to the students and their families (Mpofu et al., 2013). This study further highlighted that it became a trend throughout Africa for governments and institutions to adopt and implement policies designed to reduce costs, including reducing student social aid and scholarship, and eliminating expenditure on learning equipment. Hence, higher education institutions were asked to generate their own revenue (Hwami, 2011). This has since culminated in the institutionalisation of higher education. In other words, commodification became a reality when the government adopted human capital theory to acknowledge the economic value of higher education, with an understanding of education changing from a public good to a private one that can be purchased on the basis of the buyer's perceived need and financial capacity. The higher education institutions are organised as industries aimed at profit and operating as businesses.

The government shifted the burden of financing higher education by increasing the participation of beneficiaries and parents, meaning that students had to pay fees without government subsidy, what Hwami called, "Neoliberalism treatment of higher education as a private commodity, a traded commodity to be purchased by a consumer, a product to be retailed by academic institutions" (2011, p. 105). This scenario has further worsened the social stratification, meaning only those from socio-economically sound backgrounds could pay. A number of studies stressed the negative consequences of neoliberal principles on higher education (see for example, Hwami, 2013; Misiaszek et al., 2012; Mpofu et al., 2013; Raftopoulos & Phimister, 2004). Even the cadetship scheme whereby needy students applied to the government for loans could not rescue the students because the government did not have money, resulting in a dire situation (Mpofu et al., 2013). The majority of the population residing in the rural areas depend on subsistence farming, which in recent years has been unreliable because of sporadic rains and harsh weather conditions. Zimbabwe has reached record unemployment, leading to higher levels of poverty and consequently school dropouts.

110   *Zvisinei Moyo*

According to Misiaszek et al. (2012), the privatisation and marketisation of all amenities, including catering and accommodation services, benefited the politically connected. This has caused a selective elite-driven economy causing untold suffering in the higher education institutions of Zimbabwe. This coincided with the movement from neoliberal globalisation, what other scholars referred to as internal colonisation, and what has been termed by Ndofirepi and Cross (2014) as indigenous kleptocratic capitalism. This has been worsened by the implementation of nativist policies aimed at acquiring land, mainly commercial farms owned by Whites of European descent (Sadomba, 2011). These developments culminated in a more unequal society than prior to independence, as the rich got richer while the majority were mired in poverty, depending solely on peasant farming and other informal work, not able to send their children to higher education institutions.

Indeed, the period since 2000 has seen a series of crises causing unprecedented suffering to the ordinary citizen. The government blamed it on the ongoing economic revolution and indigenisation of the economy. Yet other analyses saw it as consolidation of power aimed at inheriting colonial privileges. Going further, this created a discourse characterised by corruption in the biting inflation, with basic goods and cash found on the Black market at exorbitant prices. This coincided with the mass exodus of experienced academics, resulting in a drop in standards. To add to the list of challenges experienced by students in higher education, fees and levies continued to rise.

Impact of Commodification and Globalisation of Knowledge Economy on the Contribution of Women

The background and funding of higher education captures the historical background of where the majority of Zimbabwean women come from, in an era where education is at the heart of development and the world is realising the importance of globalisation. Notwithstanding the various issues affecting women, the growth in higher education, accompanied by considerable variation in gender, is a step towards the visibility of the African continent as a player in the internationalisation of higher education. Expansion in higher education has brought with it new challenges, especially in declining economies and new universities faced with underfunding; but what is positive is that it has increased opportunities for prospective students to enrol in higher education institutions (Maringe, 2008). Tertiary education has been touted as critical for women's economic empowerment (OECD, 2011).

Indeed, over the years the purpose of higher education has been impacted by factors such as globalisation, commodification, and increased competitiveness which partly has been accelerated by the introduction of global ranking lists (Brunsø et al., 2012). Ranking takes something which has been hard to measure, this being education quality, and turns it into something which can be easily compared. By so doing, ranking creates the scene which allows higher education institutions and nations to create concrete goals to strive for. This has seen universities change from being social institutions into

Liberating Women's Academic Achievements 111

businesses, exchanging knowledge (McKelvey & Holmén, 2009). This is a great opportunity for those previously disadvantaged by the geopolitics of knowledge to manoeuvre in a globalised knowledge economy.

According to the OECD (2011), education in developing economies is expanding although at a narrow base; while education is a critical dimension of social inequalities, it is also an indispensable part of the solution to social inequalities. Further, the report emphasised that education can lift people out of poverty and social exclusion. With the rapidly globalising world, higher education can help the marginalised or invisible to catch up with the rest of the world through technology advancements. It assists women to unyoke the technological divide and other exclusions and rescue Africa from extinction.

Globalisation has had a significant influence on the development of higher education. "Not only has knowledge, in the form of world brands and massive (and instantaneous) data flows, become the key resource in the global economy, scientific knowledge more narrowly defined has also become highly integrated and distributed" (Gibbons et al., 2003, p. 188). Globalisation has ushered in enormous change in the production of goods, communication technology, and new knowledge (Maringe & Gibbs, 2009). Where dominance has been determined by Eurocentrism, it is now new knowledge which holds the key to economic advancement and national success (Hazelkorn, 2011). There is a possibility that in a few years to come, labelling Africa as mentally underdeveloped may be disputed.

Higher education as a public good supports dispositions to contribute to debates (Nixon, 2010), therefore improving social life and promoting social mobility of the previously disadvantaged (Moyo, 2020). Schwartz (2013) emphasised that social mobility creates a more inclusive society. This has given rise to consumer activities; for instance, Bauman (2004) argued that Western society has moved from being a production to a consumption society. Consumers are rapidly integrating themselves into the social ranks of society, which was not the case before. The development has necessitated an increase in individualisation because of opportunities enabling anyone to create their own social identity. Giddens (2011) commented on the development of modern society and said that globalisation has to a large extent changed the way we experience the world, that is, personal identity and how we interact with others. It is important to note that globalisation has rolled out profound changes throughout societies that have destabilised established institutions, rendering them out of place and phasing out geopolitics. This has impacted women, especially in the way they define themselves. This is a great opportunity for women in higher education to reconsider their personal identity and interaction with the world around them. In the consumption society, established institutions are no longer suitable for the modern society because of their unchanging behaviour (Brunsø et al., 2012). This is opening inclusive avenues for marginalised groups to contribute.

When relating the idea of consumer society and commodification of higher education, "it can be argued that the product of knowledge does not take a form of a material possession" (Brunsø et al., 2012, p. 32). Knowledge, which

112   *Zvisinei Moyo*

was once a scarce resource, is now accessible due to development of new ideas where knowledge has been multiplied and turned into a marketable product. That said, I argue that universities have been commodified due to competitiveness and ranking and, in this case, women can access knowledge by contributing to debates or consuming without any boundaries or hierarchies. This has made it possible for consumers in higher education to consume according to their own wishes and demands. This is largely necessitated by commodification and globalisation to make knowledge which was previously unreachable into something which can be accessed regardless of gender, ethnicity, or geographical location.

According to Maringe and Gibbs (2009, p. 10), "Commodification takes place when economic value is assigned to something that traditionally would not be considered in economic terms, for example, an idea, identity or gender." Commodification, as explained by Brunsø et al. (2012), consists of goods and services which are produced for exchange; exchange is monetised, and monetary transactions take place for the purpose of profit. Given the way education exchange is monetised, it has the potential to generate economic development and prosperity. Since commodification means that all production is about profit, Zimbabwean women who are grappling exclusion and marginalisation based on social relations influenced by patriarchal ideologies, can have their voices heard outside the epistemological global hierarchy of power. The focus is shifting from developing the entire society in order to improve the lives of all people to a more practical and individual purpose. Brunsø et al. (2012) indicated that knowledge is now produced and traded the same way as other goods and services in the knowledge society due to commodification. Higher education can have indirect benefits for economies (Teferra, 2014) and enable greater opportunities for economic advancement.

As universities stand at the heart of knowledge production, the number of female students has grown fairly steadily, despite the general underrepresentation. Teferra (2014, p. 15) explained the conventional dominance of Western concepts and strategies:

> The importance of the internationalisation of higher education in the era of the knowledge economy, has been growing by leaps and bounds for its anticipated contribution to quality higher education, promotion of research, regional/global integration, fostering human resource capacity.

That said, elements of internationalisation have accelerated the mobility of scholars and students regionally and internationally. Such developments are enhanced by the fast connectivity facilitated by growing technological enhancements. The quality procedures of accreditation and world ranking bodies, curricular restructuring, research creativities, publication and communication through journals and in different data bases, as well as new forms of educational delivery, usher in new challenges, prospects, and risks to the higher education systems around the globe. Although the African continent has been regarded as the weakest contributor to the global knowledge base,

Liberating Women's Academic Achievements 113

now is the time for contributions by the few women and men who have made it to be heard in the global arena. It is time to be heard outside the epistemological global power hierarchies.

Conclusion

The chapter has shown how commodification of higher education in a globalising knowledge economy enables higher education to develop economies and, above all, catch up with more technologically advanced societies. Developing countries are under pressure to contribute to the trend in the knowledge society. To sum up, it seems as if there is a cultural change, not only within institutions of higher education but also in a broader societal context. Whether or not it is in development towards a post-modern consumer society or into a new form of modernity, Eurocentrism is becoming irrelevant. Globalisation of the world has caused changes within all aspects of our lives and naturally also when it comes to higher education institutions. Thus, when discussing the idea of how the plight of women in higher education can be changed due to current developments in the world, there are several ways of connecting this to commodification and globalisation. The concepts are interlinked; they support, strengthen, and supplement each other. The influence of commodification has had a significant influence on the development of higher education over the years.

Indeed, the extent to which women can break through pervasive structures may depend on the historical background of the country. For instance, colonisation has impeded knowledge production in Zimbabwe and other so-called Third World countries, leaving women in subordinated positions because of colonial policies, patriarchal religious values, and traditional stereotypes. These and other gender-related issues have created layers of disparities adversely affecting females in all spheres of life, including levels of education. Nonetheless, the commodification of knowledge and globalisation has a substantial influence and can be used as a springboard to unyoke knowledge previously marginalised, since it seems to be the exchange value rather than the actual use value which decides the importance of knowledge. Although the chapter focussed on a single country within the African context, it raises important implications for research, policymaking, and practice in higher education. It also has the potential to serve as a springboard to develop more broad-based, multiple-method, and large-sample comparison studies that focus on women's progress.

References

Bauman, Z. (2004). *Work, consumerism and the new poor* (2nd ed.). McGraw-Hill Education.

Bezuidenhout, A., & Cillers, F. V. N. (2010). Burnout, work engagement and sense of coherence in female academics in higher education institutions in South Africa. *South African Journal of Industrial Psychology, 36*(1), 1–10.

114 *Zvisinei Moyo*

Brunsø, A. T., Jørgensen, L. T., & Viborg, S. (2012). Commodification of higher education: International Social Science Basic Studies. Unpublished doctoral thesis. Roskilde University, BA.

Chitsamatanga, B. B. (2014). An investigation into the perceptions of female academics on their career development: A comparative study of South African and Zimbabwean universities. Unpublished Master's dissertation. University of Fort Hare, South Africa.

Chitsamatanga, B. B., Rembe, S., & Rembe, N. S. (2020). Does the implementation of affirmative action promote female academics to positions of leadership? Evidence from two state universities in Zimbabwe. *Journal of Social Sciences and Humanities*, *17*(2), 171–185.

Chitsamatanga, B. B., Rembe, S., & Shumba, J. (2018a). Are universities serving lunch before breakfast through staff development programmes? A comparative study of the experiences of female academics in South Africa and Zimbabwe universities. *Women's Studies International Forum*, *70*, 79–88.

Chitsamatanga, B. B., Rembe, S., & Shumba, J. (2018b). Mentoring for female academics in the 21st century: A case study of a South African university. *International Journal of Gender and Women's Studies*, *6*(1), 52–58.

Chitsamatanga, B. B. Rembe, S., & Shumba, J. (2018c). Promoting a gender responsive organisational culture to enhance female leadership: A case of two state universities in Zimbabwe. *Anthropologist*, *32*(1–3), 132–143.

Cohen, R., & Kennedy, P. (2007). *Global sociology* (2nd ed.). Palgrave.

Coltart, D. (2008). A decade of suffering in Zimbabwe. Economic collapse and political repression under Robert Mugabe. *Development Policy Analysis*, 5, 1–24. Centre for Global Liberty and Prosperity.

Gaidzanwa, R. B. (2007). Alienation, gender and institutional culture at the University of Zimbabwe. *Feminist Africa*, *8*, 60–82.

Garwe, E. C. & Thondhlana, J. (2018). Higher education systems and institutions: Zimbabwe. *Encyclopaedia of international higher education systems and institutions*. Springer. https://doi.org/10.1007/978-94-017-9553-1_479-1

Gibbons, M., Scott, P., & Nowotny, H. (2003). *Introduction—Mode 2 revisited: The new production of knowledge*. Online. http://www.flacso.edu.mx/openseminar/downloads/gibbons.pdf

Giddens, A. (2011). *Sociology* (6th ed.). Polity.

Guzura, T. (2017). An overview of issues and concepts in gender mainstreaming. *Afro Asian Journal of Social Sciences*, *8*(1), 1–28.

Guzura, T., & Chigora, P. (2012). Gender equality in institutions of higher learning in Zimbabwe: A case of Midlands State University's experience with female advancement, 2004–2007. *Global South: Sephis E-magazine*, *8*(2), 22–28.

Hazelkorn, E. (2011). *Rankings and the reshaping of higher education*. Palgrave Macmillan.

Hwami, M. (2011). Understanding the crisis in higher education in Zimbabwe: Critical explorations. In D. Kapoor (Ed.), *Critical perspectives on neoliberal globalization, development and education in Africa and Asia* (pp. 103–120). Sense Publishers.

Hwami, M. (2013). Zimbabwe's exodus: Crisis, migration and survival. *Canadian Journal of Development Studies/Revue canadienne d'études du développement*, *34*(3), 442–444. doi: 10.1080/02255189.2013.791258

Johnston-Anumonwo, I., & Doane, D. L. (2011). Globalisation, economic crisis & Africa's informal economy women workers. *Singapore Journal of Tropical Geography*, *32*(1), 8–21. https://doi.org/10.1111/j.1467-9493.2011.00416.x

Mandina, S. (2012). Quality rural secondary school education in Zimbabwe: Challenges and remedies. *Journal of Emerging Trends in Educational Research and Policy Studies, 3*(5), 768–774.

Maringe, F. (2008). University marketing: Perceptions, practices and prospects in the less developed world. *Journal of Marketing for Higher Education, 15*(2), 129–153. https://doi.org/10.1300/J050v15n02_06.

Maringe, F. (2009). Strategies and challenges of internationalisation in HE: An exploratory study of UK universities. *International Journal of Educational Management, 23*(7), 553–563.

Maringe, F. & Gibbs, P. (2009). *Marketing higher education—Theory and practice.* Open University Press.

Marx, K. (1952). *Capital.* F. Engels (Ed.). Encyclopaedia Britannica, Inc.

Matereke, K. P. (2011). 'Whipping into line': The dual crisis of education and citizenship in postcolonial Zimbabwe. *Educational Philosophy and Theory, 44*(s2), 84–99.

McKelvey, M., & Holmén, M. (Eds.) (2009). *Learning to compete in European universities—From social institution to knowledge business.* Edward Elgar Publishing.

McLaren, P. (2005). *Capitalists and conquerors: A critical pedagogy against Empire.* Roman and Littlefield Publishers.

Misiaszek, G. W., Jones, L. I., & Torres, C.A. (2012). Selling out academia? Higher education, economic crises and Freire's generative themes. In B. Pusser, K. Kempner, S. Marginson, & I. Ordorika (Eds.), *Universities and the public sphere* (pp. 193–210). Routledge.

Moodly, A., & Toni, N. M. (2017). Accessing higher education leadership: Towards a framework for women's professional development. *South African Journal of Higher Education, 31*(3), 138–153.

Moyo, Z. (2020). Moving toward indigenisation of knowledge: Understanding African women's experiences. In K. G. Fomunyam & S. B. Khoza (Eds.), *Curriculum theory, curriculum theorising and the theoriser* (pp. 92–105). Sense Publishers.

Moyo, Z., & Perumal, J. (2018). Globalisation and the experiences of Zimbabwean female migrant teachers. *Journal of Educational Studies, 17*(1), 76–93. https://hdl.handle.net/10520/EJC-178f27376

Mpofu, J., Chimhenga, S., & Mafa, O. (2013). Funding higher education in Zimbabwe: Experiences, challenges and opportunities of the cadetship scheme. In D. Teferra (Ed.), *Funding higher education in Sub-Saharan Africa* (pp. 327–350). Palgrave Macmillan.

Mudhovozi, P., Manyange, L., & Mashamba, T. (2013). Mentors' views of supervising post graduate students undertaking research at an institution in Zimbabwe. *Journal of Social Sciences, 37*(3), 293–300.

Mugweni, R. M. (2014). Female lecturers' promotion to elevated management positions: Emerging trends in higher education institutions. *Journal of Emerging Trends in Educational Research and Policy Studies, 5*(8), 175–182.

Naicker, L. (2013). The journey of South African women academics with a particular focus on women academics in theological education. *Studia Historiae Ecclesiasticae, 39*, 325–336.

Ndebele, C., van Heerden, J., & Chabaya, A. (2013). Development and implementation of a mentoring programme at a historically disadvantaged South African university. *Journal of Social Sciences, 34*(2), 123–133.

Ndofirepi, A. P., & Cross, M. (2014). Transforming epistemologies in the postcolonial African university? The challenge of the politics of knowledge. *Journal of Education and Learning, 8*(4), 291–298.

116 *Zvisinei Moyo*

Nixon, J. (2010). *Higher education and the public good: Imagining the university.* Continuum International Publishing.

Onyido, J. A. (2013). Education and women in the era of globalisation. *The Intuition, South Carolina, USA, 4*(1), 13–19.

Organisation for Economic Co-operation and Development (OECD). (2011). *Report on the gender initiative: Gender equality in education, employment and entrepreneurship.* TALIS, OECD Publishing.

Placket, G. (2012). Introduction: Effects of global developments on gender and the legal practice. *Indiana Journal of Global Legal Studies, 20*(2), 1061–1069.

Raftopoulos, B., & Phimister, I. (2004). Zimbabwe now: The political economy of crisis and coercion. *Historical Materialism, 12*(4), 355–382.

Sadomba, Z. W. (2011). *War veterans in Zimbabwe's revolution: Challenging neo-colonialism and settler and international capital.* Weaver Press.

Schwartz, S. (2013). *The higher purpose.* Times Higher Education. Online. Available at: https://www.timeshighereducation.com/comment/columnists/the-higher-purpose/176727. article (accessed 27 November 2020).

Shober, D. (2014). Women in higher education in South Africa. *Gender Transformation in the Academy Advanc+es in Gender Research, 19,* 315–332.

Teferra, D. (2014). Charting African higher education: Perspectives at a glance. *International Journal of African Higher Education, 1*(1), 9–21.

World Bank. (2010). *Financing higher education in Africa.* World Bank.

Yang, R. (2006). The commodification of education and its effects on developing countries: A focus on China. *Journal for Enkwicklungspolitik, 22*(4), 52–69.

Zimbabwe Education Management Information System (EMIS). (2019). *Peer review report.* Association for the Development of Education in Africa (ADEA).

Zimbabwe Ministry of Primary and Secondary Education (MoPSE). (2019). *2018 Primary and secondary education statistics report.*

Zvobgo, E. F. (2014). Gender policy implementation in the promotion of women leadership in universities: A case of Midlands State University, Zimbabwe. *Zimbabwe Journal of Science and Technology, 9*(2014), 90–97.

Zvobgo, E. F. (2015). Review of impediments to women representation and participation in university leadership. *Zimbabwean Journal of Education Research, 27*(2), 288–306.

9 The Place of Universities in Africa in the Global Information Society

A Critique

J. Kundai Chingarande and Clyton Dekeza

Characteristics of the Fourth Industrial Revolution Society

The fourth industrial revolution era, also known as the 21st century society, has been viewed by Peters (2017) as a cyber-physical society. It is the age of global connections and has power to transform human life in a number of areas such as production, manufacturing and governance (Peters, 2017, p. 3). In addition, Schwab (2016) opines that the new technologies and broadband innovations in the fourth industrial revolution era diffuse faster and more widely than in the previous revolutions. He, however, cautions that the different industrial revolutions should not be viewed as separate epochs but a continuum. The fourth industrial revolution ushered in a global information society where modern technologies dominate human life. Thus Schwab (2016) comments that the fourth industrial revolution renders technology an all-pervasive and predominant part of our individual lives. He further notes that it is important that each individual is guaranteed that the new technologies of the fourth industrial revolution are there to serve humanity and not to enslave them. The call for society to embrace the new technologies associated with the fourth industrial revolution is hinged on the assumption that the technologies will improve the standard of life of the populace.

Against the technological advancement of the global information society, a question which demands an answer is: What is the role of universities in Africa in the new society? Universities the world over are viewed as critical cogs in the development of society by imparting knowledge and skills commensurate with the needs of society. With the massive changes brought by the technological advancements in the new society, universities came under pressure to produce graduates able to function in the global information society. The new society ushered in by the industrial revolution demands that students acquire problem-solving skills in order to function in the new society. African universities are therefore challenged to model their pedagogical strategies in the light of the needs of the global information society. Thus, Kupe (2019) maintains that university education should be underpinned by teaching and learning strategies that create well-educated, socially-conscious citizens, equipped with skills relevant for the era. In addition, Waghid et al. (2019) urge African universities to play a critical role as vanguards of the

DOI: 10.4324/9781003228233-9

118　*J. Kundai Chingarande and Clyton Dekeza*

transformation demanded in the fourth industrial revolution. In that light, academies are called to be active agents in the transition. In South Africa, the government and university leaders have responded positively to the fourth industrial revolution society by recommending credible teaching and learning strategies. Technologically-based pedagogic strategies in universities should aim at producing conscious and responsible citizens. Similarly, in Zimbabwe, university curricula were changed recently from Education 3.0—which emphasised three areas of university education, namely teaching, research and community service—to Education 5.0 which incorporates innovation and industrialisation as critical aspects that gel well with the fourth industrial revolution society ("Education 5.0 and Vision 2030", 2018).

To contribute meaningfully to society, Gleason (2018) suggests that universities should adopt raptured pedagogical practices where the educator and the learner engage autonomously and deliberately as equals. This is in tandem with what Paulo Freire (1986) calls the dialogical approach. This is a pedagogical approach which is emancipatory and fosters the development of critical minds in learners. The clarion call here is that in the global information society of the fourth industrial revolution African universities should not lag behind, but embrace technology to enhance teaching and learning. Thus, educators and learners should be re-skilled to use technologies in a number of ways in pursuit of transformative forms of higher education. We maintain that university teaching and learning cannot serve society effectively if universities operate as islands; instead, university knowledges should be tailor-made to respond to the demands of the fourth industrial revolution society.

Challenges Confronted by African Universities to Fulfil Their Mandate

It is undisputed that education, and universities in particular, are the powerhouses of development. They train the human capital with the requisite skills to drive the development of society. This is true with the skills requirements of the fourth industrial revolution era. African universities, however, encounter a myriad of challenges in their pursuit to fulfil their mandate of producing graduates with the requisite knowledge and skills to develop society. The challenges are, inter alia, digital divide, corruption, gender inequality and ethnic segregation. The following section will look at digital divide and the attendant challenges it presents to the African universities.

The Digital Divide

The fourth industrial revolution rendered technology an all-pervasive and predominant part of human life (Schwab, 2016). This means that educational institutions, particularly universities, should embrace information communication technologies to prepare graduates adequately for the new society. The impact of the internet on pedagogical processes and every aspect of human life is immense. Access to information and communication technologies like

Place of Universities in Global Information Society   119

computers and the internet and the ability to use them have occupied a central place in educational development. Educators and learners use the internet to acquire new knowledge and skills. For instance, the internet is used as a medium to access current resources, thereby improving the quality of work produced by both learners and educators.

While the use of information communication technologies in educational processes is the current trend, Africa, and consequently universities in Africa, face the challenge of accessing the new technologies. Fuchs and Horak (2007) lament that in terms of the digital divide, Africa is excluded from the information society. Information communication technologies are unequally distributed between the developed and underdeveloped regions in the world. Wallerstein's world system theory explains the global inequality of economic resources. Wallerstein (2000) posits that there are three categories of regions classified on the basis of economic resources; namely, the core or developed regions; the semi-periphery, which are fairly rich; and lastly the periphery, which are the poor regions. The unequal distribution of resources and hence accessibility to information and communication technologies is known as the digital divide (Bomah, 2014). According to Bomah (2014), the core or developed countries have resources and can access information communication technologies, whereas periphery regions, Africa for example, lack economic resources, hence lack access to new technologies. The digital divide, which is tilted against the periphery (Africa), presents challenges to African universities as it disadvantages learners and educators from receiving quality education. Thus, Africa's development in education and infrastructure is hindered by the digital divide. Wilson (2004) views the digital divide as an inequality in access, distribution and use of information and communication technologies between two or more populations or groups. The digital divide manifests at different levels, for example, between regions (Wallerstein, 2000), between ethnic or racial groups in the same region or country—for example, between Blacks and Whites—and also on the basis of gender and class.

Overall, the digital divide impacts negatively on universities in Africa in their efforts to impart knowledge and skills in a number of ways. For instance, lack of physical access to technology such as the internet broadband, digital mobile devices and unequal access to information and communication resources compromise the quality of education offered by African universities compared with universities in developed countries. A number of factors contribute to the disadvantaged position of Africa in terms of access to new technologies, inter alia, weak infrastructure and political instability (Hagen, 2007). The World Bank (2001) has observed that the investment needed to develop and install telecommunication infrastructure for Information and Communications Technology (ICT) hardware and software is beyond the financial capacity of most African countries. It can be inferred that African universities' knowledge delivery is greatly hampered by the technological divide. The challenges presented by the digital divide became more visible in the COVID-19 period which forced the closure of educational institutions indefinitely and saw the adoption of online teaching. While e-learning is the

120   *J. Kundai Chingarande and Clyton Dekeza*

current trend, the quality of university knowledges delivered is compromised by a number of factors, among others, lack of ICT devices on the part of learners, lack of requisite infrastructure in African universities and lack of computer literacy skills on the part of educators and learners.

In Zimbabwe, most state and private universities have resorted to e-learning and examinations administered online. This has posed insurmountable challenges, for example, power outages, internet connectivity in rural areas and cost of Wi-Fi bundles. All these factors compromise the quality of university knowledges offered by African universities. It is imperative that African governments and university leaders invest in ICT infrastructure as well as partnering with the corporate world to equip universities with the requisite technologies in order to produce graduates who fit the fourth industrial revolution society. Such interventions should take on board learners from poor backgrounds, the girl child, disabled and minority groups. The presidential computerisation scheme pioneered by the former president of Zimbabwe Comrade R. G. Mugabe was handy in this regard although lack of supporting infrastructure militated against the success of this scheme.

Epistemological Issues and Eurocentrism

African modernism is a product of European colonialism and the missionary work of Islam and Christianity in Africa (Lamola, 2017). It is undisputed that African political consciousness and social processes, including knowledge systems, have been influenced and modelled by the colonisers' epistemic system which devalues indigenous knowledge systems. Thus, Lamola (2017) questioned whether the Western knowledge categories that Africa embraces are intellectually outdated and reactionary. The truth is that the Eurocentric epistemic system is counter-productive to the cause of Africa, hence the call to unyoke African institutions of higher learning—like universities and colleges—from the clutches of colonialism. Carnoy (1974) and Ngugi wa Thiong'o (1981) proposed a decolonisation of the mind. The call for decolonising the mind is informed by the long history of colonisation of Africa by the Western powers which entrenched their knowledge systems. It is against this backdrop that scholars view the challenges bedeviling Africa as not merely political and economic but cultural and epistemic (Lamola, 2017, p. 119).

The solution to the crisis in Africa therefore calls for the deconstruction of the Eurocentric thought categories that modelled the Afro-coloniality. A paradigm shift in the philosophy of Africa and its knowledge systems is called for if Africa is to progress. An Afro post-modernist view that champions the review of current curricula in African universities should be adopted. New and relevant questions and themes relating to education in Africa should be interrogated. Africa should occupy the centre in educational discourses in African universities. Lamola (2017) has suggested a decolonisation of Africa's knowledge systems that will culminate in the rejection of the Western worldview that is currently reproduced and perpetuated by African educational

Place of Universities in Global Information Society 121

institutions, including universities (Lamola, 2017, p. 20). Colonialism and other means of promoting White supremacy affected every aspect of social life (Nwadeyi, 2016). This implies that institutions of higher learning were not spared, hence the need to reconstruct and redesign African universities' curricula to be Afro-centric. Commenting on the situation in South Africa, Heleta (2016) highlights that universities did not change much since attainment of independence with regard to transformation from a Eurocentric to an Afrocentric curriculum. He laments that although there has been a change of policies and frameworks that promote equality and equity, little if anything has changed relating to institutional cultures and epistemological traditions as well as pedagogical processes. Thus McKaiser (2016) opines that higher education institutions in South Africa remain colonial outposts up to this day.

This is true for most African countries that were colonies of Western countries. Mbembe (2016) advocates epistemological change at African universities from Eurocentrism to Afrocentrism. He posits that there is something wrong when syllabuses designed to meet the needs of colonialism and apartheid continue into the liberation era. It is imperative, therefore, that African academics rethink, restructure, and remodel the Eurocentric epistemology and pedagogies at African universities. To this end, Letsekha (2013, p. 9) has called for a fundamental overhaul of the entire epistemological model underpinning the current university curricula. There are, however, opposing forces to the transformation of African university curricula which want to maintain the status quo for personal benefits. The history of colonialism is that colonialists advance their ideology through education, mass media and religion, to mention but a few. Althusser (1970) refers to these institutions' ideological state apparatus (Giddens & Sutton, 2013). In this regard, Bunting (2006) observes that under apartheid higher education in South Africa was designed to promote the power and privilege of the ruling White minority. Furthermore, Heleta (2016) argues that one of the destructive effects of colonialism was the subjugation of local knowledge and promotion of Western epistemology. Research has shown that European scholars worked hard to erase the contribution of Africans in the creation of knowledge. For instance, there have been attempts by colonialists to link the magnificent Great Zimbabwe monuments to the Whites (Jarus, 2017). The Whites claimed that Great Zimbabwe was built by Phoenicians or groups from Asia or Europe. Whites could not believe that Africans could put up such work of quality dexterity; however, this theory has been proved wrong by African scholars (Jarus, 2017). Thus, Said (1994, p. 8) indicates that the Western European literature for the century portrayed the non-Western world and its people as inferior and subordinate and developed the view that Europe should rule other races. This truncated philosophy was engendered through the education system. Zeleza (2009, p. 114) adds that colonial universities were unapologetically Eurocentric. In the same vein, Pietsch (2013) opines that settler universities positioned themselves as towers of "universal knowledge". This myopic and epistemic violence of African knowledge systems by the colonialists serve to

122 *J. Kundai Chingarande and Clyton Dekeza*

maintain the Western hegemony decades after African countries gained political independence. Thus, Spivak (1994) asserts that epistemic violence erases the history of the subaltern and convinces them that they do not have anything to offer to the modern world. Ramonyn (2014, cited in Pillay, 2015) opines that the curriculum in African universities and colleges still reflects the colonial worldview and still reproduces and reinforces the white supremacy that there is not much to learn from Africa.

We argue therefore that the supremacy of Whites (Whiteness) entrenched in Africa through a skewed Eurocentric curriculum should be challenged by African scholars in order to unyoke African universities from epistemic violence and Eurocentrism. In this regard, Ngugi wa Thiong'o (1981, p. 93) suggests that Europe cannot remain at the centre of the universe at African universities but that Africa must be at the centre. To disentangle themselves from the Western worldview, African universities need to adopt what Zeleza (2009, p. 127) calls the deconstruction movement. The deconstruction movement seeks to eliminate injustices in society pertaining to material inequality, poverty as well as injustices in the production and distribution of knowledge (McKaiser, 2016). Deconstruction of the Western epistemology engendered in the African universities calls for African academics to be critical of the global knowledge and not to accept anything from the West without question. Deconstruction stresses the relevance of African universities' curricula to the material, historical and social environment of the communities they serve (Letsekha, 2013, p. 14). It is a wake-up call to African governments, and departments of higher education in particular, to review and redesign university curricula to address African existential problems. However, Maseremule (2015) cautions that a fundamental change in the curriculum requires academics and administrators with a decoloniality posture. Thus, the writers argue that lack of support from political leadership is one of the stumbling blocks to the transformation of African universities' curricula. Msimang (2015) argues that Africa should cut ties with colonial curricula and begin to question the relevance of the colonial knowledge system to the continent.

African academics should take advantage of the information system society ushered in by the fourth industrial revolution to research more on Africa and African knowledge systems so that Africa is put at the centre of academic discourse in African universities. Although modern society is characterised by a digital divide, among other social inequalities, a divide which is skewed against Africa and other developing countries, African academics can exploit modern technologies to remodel and enrich African universities' curricula.

Zimbabwe started the process of transforming curricula in all state universities in 2018 under the supervision of the Zimbabwe Council for Higher Education (ZIMCHE). All state universities in Zimbabwe adopted Education 5.0, a curriculum which is anchored on five pillars, namely teaching, research, community service, innovation and industrialisation (The Patriot, 2018). The thrust of Education 5.0 curriculum is to remodel the university curriculum so as to improve the quality of graduates in terms of global competitiveness.

Place of Universities in Global Information Society 123

Magaya (2018), in his article "Digital Innovations: The Real Deal", highlights that Africa lags behind in development because of multifarious factors which include slavery, colonisation and liberation struggles which saw the continent missing the first three industrial revolutions. African universities therefore require a curriculum which addresses inequalities entrenched by colonialism and slavery. It is argued that Africa is now well positioned to participate in the fourth industrial revolution which is technology- and innovation-driven. Universities, as critical cogs in the development of society, should take a lead in the transformation of curricula so that they produce highly qualified graduates who can produce goods and services and hence create employment in Africa. The government of Zimbabwe's long-term goal is to turn Zimbabwe into an upper middle-income economy by the year 2030 and universities are expected to play a leading role towards the realisation of the vision. In line with this vision, state universities' traditional tripartite curriculum, focusing on teaching, research and community service, has been remodeled to include innovation and industrialisation. In this regard, the Minister of Higher Education and Technology Professor Murwira opines that if education cannot industrialise, it is barren ("Education 5.0 and Vision 2030", 2018). The minister advocates the transformation of the state universities' curricula to reflect the new thinking. He maintains that transformation of universities' curricula should be heritage-based for universities to bring about the desired change.

There are a number of countries that have adopted a heritage-based model in curriculum change and economic transformation successfully—Japan, Germany, China, to mention but a few. A heritage-based approach calls for African universities' academics to look around their heritage and develop globally competitive curricula and economies. Thus, in Zimbabwe, Education 5.0 aims to grow industry by prioritising Science, Technology, Engineering and Mathematics (STEM) education which emphasises the use of local resources. We therefore believe that African universities can be unyoked through the implementation of a curriculum that equips students with knowledge, skills, competencies and attitudes to transform local resources into goods and services.

Chapter Summary

The chapter explored one of the contentious issues in academic circles, the relevance of curricula implemented by African universities in the context of the fourth industrial revolution. The exploration reveals that the curricula implemented by African universities is Eurocentric because of the long history of colonisation of Africa by the Western powers such as the United Kingdom, France and Germany. It became clear in this discourse that although Africa gained political independence, it is still culturally colonised; hence African knowledge systems have been relegated to the periphery while the Western knowledge system and worldview take the centre in the university curriculum. This epistemic violence entrenched by colonialism is reproduced and sustained

124 *J. Kundai Chingarande and Clyton Dekeza*

by a number of factors, inter alia, the digital divide and lack of support to transform university curricula by the political leadership and university administrators. It has been revealed that curricula should be heritage-based if educational institutions such as universities are to impact the development of Africa. Drawing inspiration from countries that reconstructed and remodeled their curricula to be problem-solving oriented and which yielded positive results, for instance China and Germany, some African countries have started transforming universities' curricula to be Afro-centric. Zimbabwe, for instance, started to implement Education 5.0 which aims to provide solutions to the existential challenges confronted by the country. Curriculum transformation which puts Africa at the centre is viewed as the panacea to Africa's challenges. At the moment, African universities produce graduates with no relevant skills to operate in the technology-driven fourth industrial society.

References

Althusser, L. (1970). Ideology and ideological state apparatuses. (Notes towards an investigation)." In *Lenin and Philosophy and Other Essays*, pp. 142–147, 166–76. New York and London: Monthly Review Press, 1971.

Bomah, K. B. (2014). Digital divide: Effects on education development in Africa. CSDF 3 L00099238 L00099238@lyit.ie

Bunting, I. (2006). 'The higher education under apartheid'. Cloete, N., Maaseu, P. Fehnel, R., Moja, T and Gibson, T. (eds). In *Transformation in higher education* (Vol. 10, pp. 35–52). Springer.

Carnoy, M. (1974). *Education as cultural imperialism*. David Mckay Company.

Education 5.0 and Vision 2030, reconfiguring Zimbabwean University degrees. (2018, 28 March). *The Patriot*.

Fuchs, C and Horak, E. (2007). Informational Capitalism and the Digital Divide in Africa. *Masaryk University Journal of Law and Technology*. 1(2):2007. ISSN 1802-5943

Freire, P. (1986). *Pedagogy of the oppressed*. The Continuum International Publishing Group.

Giddens, A., & Sutton, P. W. (2013). *Sociology* (7th ed.). Polity Press.

Gleason, N. (Ed.). 2018. *Higher education in the era of the fourth industrial revolution*. Palgrave Macmillan.

Hagen, E. (2007). *The digital divide in Africa*. VDM Verlag Dr. Mueller e.K.

Heleta, S. (2016). Decolonisation of higher education: Dismantling epistemic violence and Eurocentrism in South Africa. *Transformation in Higher Education*, *1*(1), a9. http://dx.doi.org/10.4102/the.v1i1.9

Jarus, O. (2017). *Great Zimbabwe: African City of Stone*. https://www.livescience.com/58200great-Zimbabwe.html (Accessed 20 September 2020)

Kupe, T. (2019, 19 July). Universities are key to 4IR employment. *Mail & Guardian*. https://mg.co.za/article/2019-07-19-00-universities-are-key-to-4ir-employment

Lamola, M.J. (2017). Postmodernism: Its moment, Nature and Content. *International Journal of African Renaissance Studies-Multi-Inter-and Trans disciplinarity 12*(2)110–123.

Letsekha, T. (2013). Revisiting the debate on the Africanisation of higher education: An appeal for a conceptual shift. *The Independent Journal of Teaching and Learning*, *8*, 5–18.

Place of Universities in Global Information Society   125

Magaya, D. (2018, 18 November). Digital innovations: The vision 2030 real deal. *Sunday Mail.*

Maseremule, M. H. (2015). Why Africa's professors are afraid of colonial education being dismantled. *The Conversation,* 25 November, viewed 30 November 2015, from https://theconversation.com/why-africas-professors-are-afraid-of-colonial-education-being-dismantled-50930

Mbembe, A. (2016). Decolonizing the university: New directions. *Arts & Humanities in Higher Education, 15*(1), 29–45. http://dx.doi.org/10.1177/1474022215618513

McKaiser, E. (2016). *Epistemic injustices: The dark side of academic freedom.* 2016 DCS Oosthuizen Academic Freedom Memorial Lecture, Rhodes University, Grahamstown, 30 May, viewed 17 June 2016, from http://www.iol.co.za/news/epistemic-injustices-the-dark-side-of-aca+demic-freedom-2029747

Msimang, S. (2015). The old is dying and the young ones have just been born. *Africa Is a Country,* 15 May, viewed 2 July 2016, from http://africasacountry.com/2015/05/the-old-is-dying-and-the-young-ones-have-just-been-born/

Nwadeyi, L. (2016, 29 June). We all have a responsibility to disrupt the status quo. *Mail & Guardian.* http://mg.co.za/article/2016-06-29-we-all-have-agency-and-we-must-use-it-to-disrupt-the-status-quo

Peters, M. A. (2017). Technological unemployment: Educating for the Fourth Industrial Revolution. *Journal of Self-Governance and Management Economics, 5*(1), 25–33. https://doi.org/10.22381/JSME5120172

Pietsch, T. (2013). Empire and higher education internationalisation. *University World News,* 20 July, Issue No: 282. http://www.universityworldnews.com/article.php?story=20130718115637589

Pillay, S. (2015). Decolonising the university. *Africa Is a Country.* viewed 16 June 2016, from http://africasacountry.com/2015/06/decolonizing-the-university/

Said, E. (1994). *Culture and imperialism.* Vintage.

Schwab, K. (2016). *The fourth industrial revolution.* World Economic Forum.

Spivak, G. C. (1994). Can the subaltern speak? In P. Williams & L. Chrisman (Eds.), *Colonial discourse and post-colonial theory: A reader* (pp. 66–111). Routledge.

wa Thiong'o, Ngugi. (1981). *Decolonising the mind: The politics of language in African literature.* East African Educational Publishers Ltd.

Waghid, Y., Waghid, Z., & Waghid, F. (2019). The fourth industrial revolution reconsidered: On advancing cosmopolitan education. *South African Journal of Higher Education, 33*(6), 1–9.

Wallerstein, I. (2000). *The essential Wallerstein.* The New York Press.

Wilson, E. (2004). *The information revolution and developing countries.* MIT Press.

World Bank. (2001). *World development report 2000/2001: Attacking poverty. World development report.* Oxford University Press. https://openknowledge.worldbank.org/handle/10986/11856 License: CC BY 3.0 IGO."

Zeleza, P. T. (2009). African studies and universities since independence: The challenges of epistemic and institutional decolonization. *Transition, (101),* 110–135. http://dx.doi.org/10.2979/trs.2009.-.101.110

10 Gender, Disability, Rurality, and Social Injustice in the African University
Opportunities Going Forward

Amasa P. Ndofirepi

Literature is awash with evidence of discourses about what knowledge should be included in the core curriculum of higher education institutions. The production, dissemination, teaching and advancement of knowledge are at the nucleus of higher education. While each higher education institution approaches and implements its knowledge utilities uniquely, some set standards, universal patterns and disciplinary purviews lean rigidly, stipulating the content of scientific knowledge to be learnt and how it is produced through research including the pedagogies of distributing it via teaching, publications or conferencing. However, contemporary discourses on the socially-just epistemologies place a public responsibility on institutions of higher learning, including universities, to acknowledge and value the diversity of knowledges and the embedded ways of knowing. Arguing from a holistic paradigm, an egalitarian, democratic society espouses the development of the individual along natural and ethical lines in the framework of the collective.

The purpose of this volume was to reflect on the actual teaching and learning in African higher education with the aim of achieving relevance to both African students and communities. Contributors have employed diverse approaches that have ranged from conceptual reflections to empirical investigations. These approaches have brought a theoretical and practical balance to the volume. Contributors have shown that teaching and learning in African higher education are often alienated from the existential circumstances, experiences and realities of the African student.

Contemporary debates on inclusion have revolved around the notions of multiculturalism, multicultural education and ethnic studies, to globally refer to diversity, and to articulate the representation of all perspectives from the traditionally marginalised groups that have been excluded from participation and/or have been left behind or that have traditionally been excluded from or ineffectually observed in the curriculum. Equally, there has been an incessant call for the inclusion of diverse perspectives in the curriculum. By excluding diverse perspectives in the curriculum, students' learning will be curtailed, retaining them as ill-prepared citizens in spaces that preach democracy in diversity. To exclude certain knowledges based on gender, race and physical makeup is a demonstrable show of contradictions between the rhetoric and the practice of democracy. To that end, the current emancipatory approach seeks

DOI: 10.4324/9781003228233-10

Gender, Disability, Rurality, and Social Injustice 127

to correct such social inconsistencies, leading to the contemporary calls for civil rights, women's rights and disability movements that pressured the higher education institutions to consider offering a more inclusive curriculum.

But in essence what is diversity and what purpose does it serve in society? According to Swain, the Association of American Colleges and Universities (AAC&U) defines diversity as the diversity generated in any societal structure (and inside any individual) by the existence of different perspectives and ways of making meaning, that also commonly circulate from the impact of various cultural and social heritages, discrepancies in how we socialise women and men, and disparities that arise from class, age and developed ability (Swain, 2013).

From the above, one gets the impression that diversity signifies the gamut of difference in people concerning all of the inborn and socio-cultural divergences that affect their perspectives and lived experiences including gender, race, ethnicity, sexual orientation, nationality, age, ability, class, religion, language, culture, ideas, structures and values, among other possibilities. One of the key functions of diversity is to enrich, augment and deepen the educational experiences of learners by defying categorised preconceptions while enhancing critical thinking and assisting students to learn to interconnect effectively with people of varied backgrounds. They learn from those whose experiences, beliefs and perspectives are different from their own. To that end, it would be safe to say that an obligation to plural environments is a recognition of multiplicity as dominant regimes allow for the otherness of the other.

In this book, the expanded function of the state in enhancing educational justice for individuals living with disabilities (ILDs) was discussed by arguing that facilities need to be offered for the disabled. It is through the committed engagement of both the state and members of ILDs and efficient communication lines that are inclusive and respected through reacting, authentic representation of ILDs, that this service bears fruit. Such an enhanced interaction respects rights and strengthens the dignity and livelihoods of ILDs, especially during pandemics when ILDs are likely to face double tragedies emanating from poor governance and various forms of societal exclusions. A higher education system that fails to serve ILDs' needs only perpetuates the manifestation of injustices that ILDs face, especially during the COVID-19 pandemic. A point has been made for the rights, dignity and livelihoods of the ILDs to improve through an all-inclusive education system.

The voices of students with disabilities on the provision of inclusive higher education in Africa have been echoed variously. In this book, a case has been made for the inclusion of disabled students in teaching and individual accommodation before improving infrastructure, as attempts to professionalise them are underway just like for all other students. By making available equal opportunities for the acquisition of professional skills, students with disabilities stand the chance of adding value to knowledge production in higher education. It is by listening to their voices that the world can acknowledge how their unique needs can be taken care of. A radical institutional transformation is, therefore, necessary in order that all people, including those with disabilities, can access, participate, succeed and, in turn, contribute to knowledge in higher education.

128   *Amasa P. Ndofirepi*

The provision of accessible and friendly facilities and programmes that accommodate the physically challenged students have been recommended for institutions of higher learning by stipulating specific guidelines to be followed. Infrastructural designs that contribute to the needs and interests of the disabled are suggested. By developing alternative testing procedures, and providing different educational auxiliary aids, disabled students will receive the requisite academic assistance, including tutorial sessions, extra examination time, and deadline extensions and will thus have equal access to knowledge, just like their abled peers. However, due to the massification of university education, the above policy frameworks have not done much to assist students with disabilities It was recommended that a mechanism be put in place to ensure that what is written down on paper is translated into action.

Drawing on the stratified reality analogy, the questions of equity and inclusion within the institutions of higher learning have been found to be superficial despite an increase in enrolments from students of previously disadvantaged groups. To a large extent, the question of epistemic access is still a challenge in practice evidenced by students from these groups making slower academic progress or dropping out completely from programmes. Inclusion has been misunderstood to mean the isolation of students into disability centres rather than integrating them into mainstream classes.

The *actual reality* should take into account the calls for the curriculum to be decolonised by including the indigenous knowledge systems to Africanise institutions of higher learning to enhance student cognitive justice. The stubbornness and inelasticity towards reform and change in assessment practices still favour standardisation, to the detriment of students' uniqueness and differences in learning. The *real reality* of things in African higher education points to the use of inclusion as an instrument to disregard the marginalised from actual inclusion which can make them access genuine education that may lead to their empowerment. There appears to be a deliberate, though sometimes subtle, intent to preserve intellectual dominance and power by those who enjoy the privileges of access to empowering education.

The social model of disability advocates equal participation of students with disabilities in preferred lifestyles and the accompanying appreciation of human rights for people with challenges by eliminating the barriers that disadvantage them from performing just like their peers without disabilities. Some African university environments appear as agents of exclusion as they regard themselves as ivory towers which challenged students cannot reach as they are portrayed in negative contexts. Such situations bring inequality in content delivery. The mechanical approaches to teaching learners with diverse abilities should be factored into these curricula. Universities have not reduced obstacles that enable the learners with special needs to function. Dialogical engagements on inclusivity are therefore recommended and there is a need for a more elastic curriculum that accommodates the needs of the disabled. For more epistemic justice, it is therefore recommended that the voices of learners with special needs be represented in curriculum formulations and design.

Gender, Disability, Rurality, and Social Injustice 129

African universities have not shown a reflective interpretation of the condition of being deaf as they continue to rely on the Western-centric pathologic model that views deafness as a disability in need of remedying. By patronising the deaf aspirants to university education, they continue to claim that deaf people are physiologically subordinate to hearing people. In effect, African universities have tactlessly discounted their context of protest and struggle against colonialism by standing at the forefront of acknowledging diversity and social justice. It is therefore recommended that higher education practices, including the provision of knowledge, should encompass the African ethic of ubuntu in which personhood is invested by wrestling to provide for disability in general and the condition of being deaf in particular. African universities should steer clear of the colonial view of deafness as a communication disability. It is recommended that the African notion of personhood should be the basis on which university governance is built on the view that at least some deaf students ought to be deemed as culturally Deaf rather than deaf and disabled. Such a standpoint would privilege deaf epistemologies among other diverse epistemologies, and would support human-centred philosophies and practices that decolonise education for this group of students. It can thus be concluded that an emancipatory decolonising curriculum in African universities should permit inclusivity and liberation that rejoices and embraces diversity rather than absorption; one that is for decolonisation rather than the colonising of others.

Female voices that have been encountered in an African university and beyond have been marginalised. A decolonised African university and the knowledges therein need to be calibrated to mirror an unblemished consideration of how complex subjectivities such as gender have been composed and sustained in knowledge production and dissemination. The hegemonic power matrix has an impact on the epistemic realm by delineating the knowledge and knowing of marginalised people, including women, as deficient and insignificant, if not unsubstantive. It is only by reclaiming their position in the academy that women in African universities can repossess epistemic recognition to guarantee themselves epistemic and ontological justice.

The condition of knowledge production and dissemination in African universities is limiting as far as knowledge democracy is concerned with the gender factor weighing against it as women struggle to unyoke the voices of women academics. The epistemic injustices that continue to manifest themselves in knowledge production and circulation in the university are characterised by the lack of access and active participation of women in the curriculum, research and positions of power. Despite remedial steps through affirmative action strategies and policies, the need for more concerted efforts to monitor and enforce them will safeguard the total emancipation of women in higher education. It is recommended that women should themselves eschew intraconflict and provide for each other if they are to overcome the obstructions to knowledge democracy and justice.

The notion of the commodification of knowledge in a globalising knowledge economy has established itself in higher education and characterised by

130   *Amasa P. Ndofirepi*

efforts to draw near the more technologically-advanced societies. The pressure is now on developing countries to contribute to the global trend in the knowledge society. This has led to a cultural change within institutions of higher education but also in a broader societal context. Globalisation of the world has triggered changes within all aspects of the generality of humanity, including its recognised penetration into higher education institutions. While women can break through pervasive structures, the colonisation of countries in the Global South has impeded knowledge production and has left women in inferior positions due to colonial policies, patriarchal religious values and traditional stereotypes. These and other gender-related issues have created layers of disparities adversely affecting females in all spheres of life, including levels of education. A re-visioning of the commodification of knowledge and globalisation mantra can be a springboard for unyoking previously marginalised knowledge.

The trend of women's positioning, leadership and enrolment were examined in this book by comparing and contrasting the Rwandan and South African higher education systems. Despite noting the progress made in the two countries thus far, there is enhanced advocacy for the advancement of men in South African and women in Rwandan higher education. More specifically, it is recommended that there be more advocacy for women enrolment and positioning in Rwandan higher education, while simultaneously advocating the increased enrolment of men in South African universities, especially at undergraduate levels and postgraduate level up to Master's level. In the same vein, as academics endeavour to be enrolled at the PhD level and to receive senior management positions, associate professorship and full professorship, there are clear indicators of enhanced educational injustices towards women. It is also proposed that the model of critical feminist transnational praxis can serve as a model across borders and across countries, where countries can create praxis wetlands or "praxis zones" where researchers, activists, community groups, educators, policy-makers and other stakeholders gather to identify and confront any social or educational injustices. Gender equity and gender parity at all levels of education, with particular emphasis on higher education, is called for; education is supposed to serve as a driver for development.

The polemical academic discourses on the relevance of curricula implemented by African universities in the context of the fourth industrial revolution were explored in this book. The Eurocentric canons rooted in the long history of colonisation of Africa by the Western powers continue to show their ugly head in African universities long after the attainment of political independence, with traditional knowledge systems relegated to the periphery while centring scientific Western knowledges in the university curriculum. This epistemic violence entrenched in colonialism is replicated in several issues like the digital divide and lack of support to transform university curricula by the political leadership and university administrators. It has been revealed that curricula should be heritage-based if educational institutions such as universities are to impact the development of Africa. Contemporary

Gender, Disability, Rurality, and Social Injustice 131

African universities produce graduates deficient of the relevant skills to operate in the fourth industrial society which is technology-driven. Strides towards curriculum change in higher education in some African countries include the implementation of Education 5.0 which aims to provide solutions to the existential challenges confronted by the country. Curriculum transformation which puts Africa at the centre is viewed as the panacea for Africa's challenges.

Reference

Swain, S. G. (2013). Diversity education goals in higher education: A policy discourse analysis. *Electronic Theses and Dissertations, Paper 1957*. https://digitalcommons. library.umaine.edu/etd/1957

Afterword

Yusef Waghid

It is an ambitious, yet justifiable intellectual effort to bring decolonisation, an African university, and knowledge(s) in and about diversity and plurality into conversation. The very notion of decolonisation implies an intellectual resistance against forms of subversive and colonised knowledge(s). How else would one classify knowledge produced through colonising ambitions which invariably undermines legitimate forms of knowledge? Any political action aimed at subjugating knowledge cannot be considered as legitimate because its premise is undergirded by the notion of exclusion. In this way, decolonisation as an intellectual pursuit to oppose hegemonic forms of knowledge aimed at marginalisation, indoctrination, and exclusion ought to be considered as justifiable on the basis that it challenges forms of knowledge production aimed at domestication and assimilation of indigenous communities. Consequently, the intellectual endeavours by contributors in this volume ought to be lauded for the epistemological courage to subvert dominant and exclusive forms of knowledge production and dissemination.

If a university ought to be considered as an intellectual pedagogical space where knowledge is construed, advanced, and disseminated, then it ought to be tenable to link the idea of a university to its contextual underpinnings. The view that a university ought to be regarded as the intellectual space where universal knowledge is produced and, any scholarly attempt to link it to the context of Africa should be avoided, rests on a spurious assumption that knowledge in Africa is too barbaric and irrelevant to have any significant impact on the formation of the idea of a university. Undeniably, any society, is heterogeneous and consequently its knowledge claims would be contentious, contestable, and diverse. Some knowledge claims are local or indigenous whereas other claims are external to what might be localised forms of knowledge. And, what lies external to the local forms of knowledge might either be global or universal. Invariably then, what seems to happen in heterogeneous societies is an effort to bring what is local into deliberation with what counts as universal or global. In this way, an African university cannot be denied of engaging with the universal, and any attempt at minimising its legitimate claims to engage with universal knowledge, undermines an African university's legitimate standing as a universal institution of higher knowledge production. Throughout the volume the contributors are legitimately

Afterword 133

concerned with proffering that accentuate the universal knowledge claims of an African university.

The most significant contribution of this volume lies in laying bare what constitutes plura-versal knowledge—a matter of bringing the local into deliberation with what is conceived as universal—and its ramifications for African thought and practice. Likewise, its novelty is enhanced by tackling issues of gender, (dis)ability, (dis)advantage, and rurality enframed within a paradigm of epistemic justice. Epistemic justice is possible when epistemological inclusion, democratization, and unconditional autonomy are aspired towards in relation to knowledge and, which the decolonising intellectual efforts in this volume attest to. In the first, place, epistemological inclusion recognises that many forms of knowledge are authentic if such knowledges are justified for their reasoned and not so reasoned assertions. If assertions are not so reasoned it means that the justifications proffered are not always as convincing as might be or become. But, this does not mean that assertions are inauthentic and irrelevant. Rather, such claims remain in becoming. Secondly, democratisation of knowledge, so evident in the volume, is a recognition that multiple knowledge claims are brought into critical scrutiny and argued for in ways that are plausible enough for recognition and authenticity. The point is disparate knowledge claims are being contested and taken into dissonance. How else, should knowledge be produced? Finally, the freedoms of intellectuals to speak their minds and to come to speech is a vindication that an African university is alive and well and that knowledge construction, reconstruction, and deconstruction ought to remain the epistemological conceptual tools that constitute what it means to be a university. This volume written in defence of an African university with plura-versal knowledge claims, does not disappoint and summons readers to engage with what is other, different, and African!

Index

Page numbers in *Italics* refer to figures; **bold** refer to tables.

Abbott, A. 23
academic publishing 86
actual domain 40–41
actual reality 128
African modernism 120
African universities: challenges in 118; in curriculum and research 1–2; digital divide 6, 118–120; epistemological issues and Eurocentrism 120–123; fourth industrial revolution society 117–118; gender, disability, rurality, and social injustice in 6, 126–131; social exclusion 2
Afrocentric principle 48
Afrocentrism 74
Akala, B. 4, 85, 87, 91
Alkire, S. 11
all-hands-on-deck strategy 72
Althusser, L. 121
Alwy, A. 2
American Sign Language (ASL) 60
Anderson, E. 86
Andrews, J. F. 53
Artiles, A. J. 42
Arvin, M. 76
Asher, N. 73–74
assistive technologies 16
Association of American Colleges and Universities (AAC&U) 127
Atanga, L. L. 71
audism 55

Badge, J. 25
Baumann, H. D. L. 55
Bauman, Z. 111
Berghs, M. 57
Bernstein, B. 45
Bezuidenhout, A. 104

Bhaskar, R. 48
Bigge, M. L. 24
Black feminism 76–77; epistemology 78–79; movement, in scholarship 69
Bomah, K. B. 119
Boughey, C. 40, 48
Brown, P. M. 62
Brunsø, A. T. 112
Buchanan, A. 9–10
Budig, M. 87
Bunting, I. 121
Butler, J. 72

capability approach 17
capitalist accumulation model 107
Carnoy, M. 120
Cedillo, S. 76
Cerasnova, Z. 48
Chabaya, O. 98
Charlton, J. I. 53
Chimedza, R. 53, 59
Chingarande, K. 6
Chitsamatanga, B. B. 86, 94, 97, 99
Cillers, F. V. N. 104
Clough, P. 43
Coetzee, A. A. 68, 75
cognitive justice, in higher education 44–45
Cohen, R. 108
Collins, P. H. 69; Afrocentric feminist epistemology 78; cognition 69; creation of knowledge 79; omission, trivialisation, and depoliticisation 69
colonialism 55, 64, 70, 76
commodification, of higher education 45
commodification, of knowledge 5, 103, 105, 107–108; economy impact of 110–113; in globalising knowledge economy 129–130

Index 135

community of practice 55
Connell, R. W. 70–71
constant comparative analysis 26
Constitution of Zimbabwe 14
Convention of the Rights of Persons with Disability 40
Cooper, R. 63
Corbett, J. 43
COVID-19 lockdown, disability injustice 15–19
critical feminist theory 87–89
critical realism 40–41, *42*
Cross, M. 40, 48–49, 110

Deaf epistemology 62
Deaf gain 55
deafness 4; Deaf epistemology 62–63; Deaf *vs.* deaf 52; disability 53–56; epistemic accessibility, for Deaf students 59–60; historical/psychological and literary knowledge 63; medical/pathological understanding of 56, 60–62; social model 56–57; socio-cultural model 58–62; sociological and anthropological knowledge 63; Western-centric pathologic model 129
decolonial theory 32
decolonisation 70, 74, 120; feminists' voices in 75–79
decolonisation of the mind (wa Thiong'o) 2
Dei, G. J. S. 77
Dekeza, C. 6
Department of Education 39
Department of Higher Education and Training 25
deprivations 11
de Saxe, J. 87–88
Devlieger, P. J. 53, 58–59
Diagnostic and Statistical Manual 54
dialogical approach 118
Dickson, B. 23
digital divide 118–120
disability 43, 53; *see also* deafness; centres 3, 43, 46; medical model 54; social model 54–57; traditional moral model 53, 55–56
disability justice, in education 9–11; COVID-19 lockdown contributed to 15–19
Disability Resource Units 61–62
Disability Unit (DU) 26, 46
Disabled People's International (DPI) 57

discrimination 18
Divala, J. 87
diverse perspectives, in curriculum 126–127
Doane, D. L. 108
Dotson, K. 79
Dunne, M. 89–92

economic challenges 14
Education 5.0 curriculum 118, 122
Education programme 22, 27, 30
education rights, state obligation and duties in 13–15
Edwards, S. 58
Ellison, C. 43
empirical domain 40–41
epistemic injustices 129
epistemic justice 75
epistemic violence 122
epistemological access 16, 48
equitable learning 44–45
equity of epistemologies 45
Eriksen, E. O. 11
ethical standards 24
Eurocentric curriculum 39
Eurocentric epistemic system 120
Eurocentric modernity, through colonialism and imperialism 1
Eurocentrism 73–74, 111; epistemological issues and 120–123
exclusion 18, 22, 29–30, 40
extractivism 12

Fanon, F. 74
Farganis, S. 71
Farman, R. 22
feminist epistemic struggle 86, 89–90; *see also* knowledge democracy; higher education and 90–98; women's empowerment, pathways to 98–100
feminist standpoint theory 70
feminist voices, in African University curriculum 4; curriculum reforms 73–75; decolonisation 75–70; ideologies/belief system 71; overview of 68–70; subjectivities, theorising feminisms and arguments on 70–73
Fitchett, A. 35
formal access 16, 48
Foucault, M. 53–54
fourth industrial revolution society, characteristics of 117–118
Freedman, J. 71
Freire, P. 118
Fuchs, C. 119

136   *Index*

Garberoglio, C. L. 62
Garwe, E. C. 108
Gaztambide-Fernández, R. A. 75
Geisinger, B. N. 88
gender complementarity 78
gender equity 103–104, 130
gender parity 130
Gerrard, L. C. 41
Getzel, E. E. 33
Gibbs, P. 112
Giddens, A. 111
Gleason, N. 118
globalisation, of knowledge 5, 103, 108, 130; economy impact of 110–113
Graham, L. J. 43
Grande, S. 70
Greyling, E. 29, 33
Gubrium, J. F. 26

Haralambos, M. 24
Hauser, P. C. 60
Heleta, S. 121
heritage-based model 123
higher education (HE), in Africa 85, 88–89, 99; gender and curriculum in 91–93; gender and power positions in 95–98; gender and research in 93–95
Hlatshwayo, M. N. 45
Hockings, C. 48
Holborn, M. 24
Holcomb, T. K. 62
Holstein, J. A. 26
homogenisation, of women's experiences 71
Horak, E. 119
Hosking, D. L. 29, 35
Howell, C. 33
Humphries, T. 60

Icaza Garza, R. A. 78
ILD *see* individuals living with disability (ILD)
inclusive education, in higher education 3–4, 39–40; critical realist lens 40–41, *42*; higher learning institution development 46–47, *47*; implementation 44–46; social justice and 41–43, *42*; teaching and learning strategy 47–48
inclusive pedagogy 44
individualistic medical approach 54
individuals living with disability (ILD) 2–3, 8–9, 127; COVID-19 lockdown 8, 15–19; disability justice, in education 9–11; obligations and duties 13–15;

recommendations, well-being of 18–19; structural injustice 11–13
infirmity model, of deafness 54, 56
Information and Communications Technology (ICT) 119–120
institution-based support team 46–47
International Classification of Disease ICD-10-CM 54
International Classification of Impairments, Disabilities and Handicaps (ICDH) 54

Jackson S. 87, 89
Johnston-Anumonwo, I. 108
Jones J. 89
Jones, K. 87
Jugov, T. 11–12
justice, in education 9–10

Kabzems, V. 53, 59
Kaplan, D. 53, 55
Keifer-Boyd, K. 10
Kelsen, H. 9
Kennedy, P. 108
Kenya's Vision 2030 68
Khader, S. J. 77
knowledge: commodification of 103, 105, 107–108, 110–113, 129–130; defined 84, 86; democracy *see* knowledge democracy; economy and equity 45; globalisation of 103, 108, 110–113, 130
knowledge democracy 5; *see also* feminist epistemic struggle; conceptualising feminist epistemology 86; and feminist epistemic struggle 89–91; overview of 84–86; theoretical framework 87–89
Kumalo, S. H. 45
Kupe, T. 117

Lamola, M.J. 120
Lane, H. 54
Lave, J. 55
Lazreg, M. 78
Letsekha, T. 121
Lotz-Sisitka, H. 40, 48
Lovet, T. 74

Macdonald, K. M. 23
Magaya, D. 123
Makoelle, T. M. 3
Mallory, B. L. 53
Mama, A. 71–73, 77
Mangolothi, B. 84, 96
Manombe-Ncube, J. 57

Mareva, R. 99
Maringe, F. 112
Martin, J. 87
Maseremule, M. H. 122
Masitera, Erasmus 2
Matereke, K. P. 107
Mateta, A. 15, 18
Mathieu, D. 9–10
Mbembe, A. 121
Mbiti, J. 58
McKaiser, E. 121
Medicine and Law 24
Menkiti, I. A. 58–59
Mignolo, W. 75
Ministry of Higher and Tertiary Education, Science and Technology Development 106
Ministry of Primary and Secondary Education (MoPSE) 105
Mirza, H. S. 69
Misiaszek, G. W. 110
Mladenov, T. 57
Mohanty, C. 70–71, 76–77
Moores, D. F. 63
Morrow, W. 16
Moyo, A. 15
Moyo, Z. 5, 108
Msimang, S. 122
Mugabe, R. G. 120
Muller, J. 24
Munoz-Baell, I. M. 54
Murray, J. M. 55
Musengi, Martin 4
Mutanga, O. 40

Nadar, S. 78
Naicker, L. 87, 94
National Research Foundation (NRF) 93, 104
native feminist theories 77
Ndebele, C. 100
Ndlovu-Gatsheni, S. 12, 28, 55, 59
Ndlovu, S. 3
Ndofirepi, A. P. 6, 110
neoliberal globalisation 107, 110
neoliberalism 57
Nhundu, V. 59
Njaya, T. 90, 92, 98
normalisation 54
Nussbaum, M. C. 71
Nxumalo, F. 76
Nyamnjoh, F. B. 74

Odendaal-Magwaza, M. 22
Odora Hoppers, C. A. 45

Organisation for Economic Co-operation and Development (OECD) 111
Owen, D. 12
Oyewumi, O. 71–72

Paatsch, L. E. 62
Padden, C. 60
Parekh, S. 11
Parsons, Talcott 54
participation 61
pathological model, of deafness 54, 56, 60–61
Paul, P. V. 63
pedagogy of solidarity 75
Perumal, J. 108
Peta, C. 15
Peters, M. A. 117
Peters, S. 53
philosophy of life 48, 58
Pietsch, T. 121
Placket, G. 108
Polat, F. 41
post-colonialism feminist theory 73
post-1994 transformation trajectory goals (South Africa) 68
privatisation, of higher education 45
professional judgement 24
professional knowledge: in education **25**, 25–26; in higher education 23–25; types of 25, **25**
proficiency, in english 24
psycho-medical model 43

Rahnema, M. 1–2
Ramohai, J. 87, 93
Rawls, J. 12
Reagan, T. 58, 60, 62
real domain 40–41
real reality 128
reification 61
resilience 44
Riddel, S. 27
Rowe, A. D. 48
Ruiz, T. M. 54
Runté, R. 25

Sabzalian, L. 77
Said, E. 121
Sayed, Y. 89–92
Schech, S. 2
Scheetz, N. A. 62
Scheffler, S. 9
Schiwy, F. 70, 77–78
Schneider, M. 34

138   *Index*

school/departmental-based support
    team 46–47
School of Education 30, 32, 34–35
Schwab, K. 117
Schwartz, S. 111
Shaeffer, S. 41
Shalem, Y. 23–24
Shava, G. N. 100
Shermis, S. S. 24
Shober, D. 94
Shulman, L. 25
Siple, L. A. 56
Slee, R. 43
Sleeter, C. E. 70
Smith, D. 74
social injustice 11–12
social justice 41–43, *42*, 77
socially-just epistemologies 126
social model, of disability 54–57, 128
socio-cultural model: of deafness 58–62;
    epistemic accessibility 60
socio-economic systems 93
sociological model 43
Spivak, G. C. 122
stigmatisation 57, 59
Stone, E. 53
structural constraints 44
structural injustice, for ILDs 8, 11–13, 15–16
The Structuring of Pedagogic Discourse
    (Bernstein) 45
students with disabilities' voice 3; built
    environment 30–32; entry-level
    requirements 33; equalisation of
    opportunities 27–28; improvement, of
    teaching standard 28–30;
    methodology 26–27; overview of
    22–23; physical structures 34–35;
    professional knowledge, in education
    23–26, **25**; self-advocacy 33–34
subjectivities, theorising feminisms and
    arguments on 70–73
Swain, S. G. 127
Swart, E. 29, 33
Swartz, L. 34

Taylor, G. 25
Teaching and Learning Committee 47
teaching practice, students' voices to
    improve 28–30
technologically-based pedagogic
    strategies 118

Teferra, D. 106, 112
Test, D. W. 33
Thoma, C. A. 33
Thondhlana, J. 108
Titchkosky, T. 35
transculturality 74
Tyatya, K. 93, 95

Under the Western Eye (Mohanty) 71
United Nations Convention on the
    Rights of People with Disabilities
    (UNCRPD, 2006) 58
United Nations Educational, Scientific
    and Cultural Organisation
    (UNESCO) 13–14, 17, 58
United Nations Sustainable Development
    Goal (UN SDG) 4, 52, 58
Universal Declaration of Human Rights
    Charter of 1948 (UDHRC) 13
universalisation: of knowledge 71–72; of
    women's experiences 71
universal knowledge 121

Visvanathan, S. 44
Vurayai, Simon 5

Waghid, Y. 117–118
Wallerstein, I. 6, 119
Walton, E. 45, 48
wa Thiong'o, Ngugi 55, 120, 122
Weedon, C. 71
Wenger, E. 55, 61
Western-centric pathologic model 129
Western epistemology 121–122
White Paper 6, 39
Wilson, E. 119
Winch, C. 26
Wodak, R. 71
women's empowerment, pathways to
    98–100
Woodhull, W. 77
Woodward, J. 52
World Bank (2001) 119
World Programme of Action
    Concerning Disabled Persons 57
world system theory 6, 119

Yang, R. 103, 107
Young, I. M. 11
Young, M. 24
Ypi, L. 11–12

Zeleza, P. T. 121–122
Zimbabwean higher education 103–105; commodification 107–108; economic and political demise of 106–107; funding and financing of 108–110; purpose and development 105–106; women contribution 110–113
Zimbabwe Council for Higher Education (ZIMCHE) 122
Zimbabwe Open University (ZOU) 99

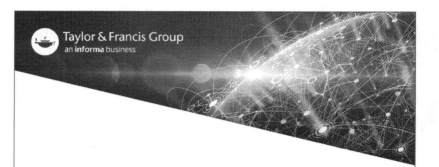